# FIVE MINUTES TO A HIGHER SALARY

*Over 60 Brilliant Salary Negotiation Scripts for Getting More*

# LEWIS C. LIN

With Christine Ko

## ALSO BY LEWIS C. LIN

*Decode and Conquer: Answers to Product Management Interviews*

*Interview Math: Over 50 Problems and Solutions for Quant Case Interview Questions*

*Rise Above the Noise: How to Standout at the Marketing Interview*

This book is dedicated to my Dad. He exposed me to the world of negotiation by getting great deals on the family car.

Patience is a crucial ingredient for any negotiation. He had a near infinite supply with excellent negotiation outcomes to match. Love you Dad.

*Lewis C. Lin*

Published by Impact Interview, 677 120th Ave NE, Suite 2A-241, Bellevue, WA 98105.

Corporations, organizations and educational institutions: bulk quantity pricing is available. For information, contact lewis@impactinterview.com.

FIRST EDITION

Lin, Lewis C.
Five Minutes to a Higher Salary: Over 60 Brilliant Salary Negotiation Scripts for Getting More in Just Five Minutes / Lewis C. Lin.

# Table of Contents

# PART 3 SALARY NEGOTIATION SCRIPTS FOR CANDIDATES

# Introduction
## Why did you write a book on salary negotiations?

I love winning. Not a little. A lot.

Ask my kid sister. Growing up, we watched the movie, *The Karate Kid*, over and over. The movie's villain, Cobra Kai, had a "no mercy" rule. I took no mercy too literally with my sister. Every time we played Monopoly, I would beat her to a pulp. Sorry sis. I now realize that not every four-year-old likes to get beaten by her eleven-year-old brother, even if it was just a board game.

Decades later, I would like to think I have matured since my early board gaming days. But I will admit. I still hate losing, especially in negotiation.

After a few unsuccessful negotiations, I obsessed over how I could be a better negotiator. I enrolled at Northwestern University's Kellogg School of Management and began my formal negotiation training. I then applied my negotiation skills in cities like Shanghai, Rome, and Istanbul.

Then, partnering with Christine Ko, a main contributor to the book, we started a company: Salary Boost (http://gosalaryBOOST.com). Salary Boost is a salary negotiation service. Job candidates can hire Salary Boost to write their salary negotiations scripts and get more money. Here are some of our favorite salary negotiation wins:

- Several years ago, we negotiated an *82% salary increase* for a technology executive at a Fortune 500 company.
- Last year, we negotiated a $20,000 base salary increase for a banking executive at one of Canada's top banks.
- A few months ago, we negotiated a $40,000 increase in total compensation for a candidate joining one of the hottest startups in Silicon Valley.

- And last week, we helped a new college graduate get an extra $10,000 in base salary at her dream company. She had no competing offers.

*Five Minutes to a Higher Salary* is our salary negotiation handbook. It is our go-to resource for an upcoming salary negotiation. We are delighted to share this resource with you; it encompasses everything we have practiced and learned about salary negotiation.

## What does this book have that other negotiation books do not?

There are many negotiation books. Here is why we think this book deserves a place on your bookshelf.

### Focus on SALARY negotiation

Other negotiation books cover a range of negotiation settings from buying a car to getting your kids to sleep. Negotiation concepts from one domain can be applied to be another. But it is not always clear how a real estate negotiation might work for salary. So we decided not to tell those stories and waste your time.

### A book you will actually USE

Many negotiation books are theoretical in nature. These books detail scientifically-researched principles and theories. But when it is time to get better salary negotiation outcomes, the burden shifts from the author to the reader. The reader is responsible for translating principles and theories into actionable steps. And it is not easy.

Our approach is different. This book has over 60 salary negotiation scenarios. Flip to that section for guidance, and use the scripted email and phone templates.

In other words, we are focused on getting you positive negotiation outcomes, quickly, based on recent negotiation research.

### FAST results, with a focus on what to say

If you are like the rest of us, you probably do not negotiate often. As consumers, we are accustomed to paying set prices for goods and services. And there is a good reason for this: It would be unnecessarily time-consuming if consumers haggled over every purchase – big or small.

If you are reading this book, you need results now. And we are confident that you can get results in five minutes or less.

*Five Minutes to a Higher Salary* will never leave you guessing how to apply a negotiation concept to get what you want. We get results quickly by telling you exactly what you need to say at the negotiation. The book is oozing with countless scripts and specific phrases that you, if you wish, can cut-and-paste directly into emails or mimic in a phone or face-to-face negotiation.

Our goal is not to teach you negotiation theory. Rest assured, each technique and script we recommend is supported with concepts and reasoning from leading academic centers on negotiation research. We just won't bore you with pedantic details. At the end of the day, we would like you to judge the book on whether you received a higher salary, not whether you received a good grade on the negotiation class exam.

## How to Get the Most Out of this Book

*Five Minutes to a Higher Salary* is best used as a reference book. The book is not written like a novel. In other words, it is not meant to be read cover-to-cover over a single weekend.

Here is how we would recommend using the book:

### Part 1: Negotiation Basics

If you are new to negotiation or need a refresher, read this short section on negotiation basics. You will learn more about:

- Getting comfortable with negotiating

- Figuring out what you want
- Preparing for the negotiation
- Winning the negotiation

If you are a negotiation expert or you have recently read several negotiation books, you can skip this section.

**Part 2: Frequently Asked Questions**

In this section, you will find over 30 frequently asked questions about salary negotiation. Do not skip this valuable and popular section. Get answers to your most urgent and puzzling negotiation questions.

**Part 3: Salary Negotiation Scripts for Candidates**

Go to the table of contents. Find the salary negotiation scenario that applies to your individual case, such as negotiating with a competing offer or negotiating without upsetting your manager.

Flip to the applicable section. Read the scenario and see if it is similar to your situation. Grasp the recommended solution.

If you are negotiating over email, modify the email negotiation script to suit you. For instance, replace the fictitious company names and substitute with names and details from your own situation. And if you would like to inject your own personality into the script, adjust the tone of voice with your own style. In case you are curious, email negotiation is just as acceptable as phone negotiation. In Part 2, we discuss phone vs. email negotiation in more detail.

If you are negotiating over phone or face-to-face, add two more steps to the suggestion in the previous paragraph. First, practice your script verbally. Rehearse your lines in the bathroom or when you are commuting to work. Verbal practice helps you feel more comfortable and minimizes the likelihood that you get choked up during the actual negotiation.

Second, role play the negotiation with a friend. Have your friend play the other party. After a few practice role plays, you will feel more comfortable negotiating.

During the role play, invite your friend to pepper you with potential rebuttals and counterarguments. Also ponder and write a list of anticipated objections and questions, along with your response, in advance.

## Part 4: Salary Negotiation Scripts for Recruiters and Hiring Managers

Part 4 is organized in the same manner as Part 3, but it is intended for recruiters and hiring managers.

So recruiters and hiring managers, just like Part 3, find the appropriate scenario, modify the script to your own style and situation, and rehearse before the actual negotiation. You will get far better outcomes if you are prepared. The candidate will feel more comfortable as well, increasing chances that the candidate will join your company. Do not forget to rehearse your discussion with a co-worker.

## Appendix

We also included a generous appendix filled with more resources for your upcoming negotiation including:

- **Power Phrases**. Don't need a script, but need to figure out how to word your negotiation request? We include dozens of bite-sized phrases to phrase your negotiation ask correctly.
- **Glossary**. See a negotiation term that you are not familiar with? Refer to our glossary of common negotiation terms.
- **Negotiation Documents**. We have a variety of templates to help you prepare for your next negotiation including negotiation preparation worksheets and performance review sheets.

## There are TWO Magic Scripts You Do Not Want to Miss

After we drafted an early manuscript of *Five Minutes to a Higher Salary*, one of our reviewers asked, "What's the easiest, super-simple way to get more money?" It was a great question. It made us think harder about how to make the salary negotiation process even easier for you, while getting results.

This feedback led us to create two magical scripts. The first script will help you get a better JOB OFFER in under ONE minute. The second script will help you get a RAISE in less than TWO minutes. With perhaps thousands of dollars on the line, we cannot think of another script, document or email that can achieve a better ROI per minute as these two magical scripts.

Of course, we do want you to read the entire book, so we have strategically placed both scripts at the end of the book, filed under Resource G and H. For those of you who flip ahead, we do not blame you. You do not want to miss these two scripts.

## One More Thing

We are always interested in hearing from readers. To send a note, ask a question, or report typos just email lewis@impactinterview.com.

Enjoy the book. There is no time to waste. Boost your salary now.

*Lewis C. Lin, with Christine Ko*
*January 2015*

# Part 1 Negotiation Basics

Read on if you are looking for a refresher on negotiation basics. Otherwise, you are welcome to skip this section and go directly to the negotiation scripts.

# Getting Ready to Negotiate
## Salary negotiations start sooner than you expect

We mistakenly believe negotiations begin after the interview process, when we are about to get a job offer. So we put off thoughts of negotiation until after then. However, the first step in salary negotiations happens well before that. It happens with the first call with your recruiting contact, when the recruiter asks the seemingly innocuous question, "What is your current and expected salary?"

Unbeknownst to many salary negotiators, what you say next will have a big consequence on how your salary negotiation unfolds. Later on, we will have thorough guidance on how to answer the "What is your current and expected salary?" question.

Focusing on the now, the takeaway we would like you to have is this: anytime during the beginning, middle, or end of a job search process or career discussion, there is a negotiation happening. You need to be prepared.

## Be comfortable with negotiating

More likely than not, you find negotiating unpleasant. It is natural to feel that way. Here are reasons why we do not like to negotiate:

- **Do not know how to negotiate**. We often know that we should negotiate, but we do not know how. Or how to do it effectively. Last thing we want to do is to negotiate incorrectly and not get what we want. Or worse, negotiate and look foolish in the process.
- **Hate confrontation**. There is a rare minority that is comfortable with requesting what they want. But for the vast majority of us, speaking up and making a request feels icky.

Why? It makes us feel awkward. If they reject our request, we might feel ashamed for asking. The other party might also make us feel guilty about our request. They might say nasty things like, "Wow, I'm shocked you are not satisfied with our compensation. I guess you are all about the money."

- **Worry about relationships**. We might talk ourselves out of asking for what we want. We justify those actions by saying, "I'd hate to have a poor relationship with my boss by requesting an extra $10,000."

Despite our fears, here are three reasons why we should negotiate:

- **Employers expect you to negotiate**. According to a Salary.com survey, 84 percent of employers expect candidates to negotiate salary once an offer has been made.
- **You will miss out on tangible financial upside**. Margaret Neale, a Stanford University professor, points out that even with a modest $7,000 salary increase, compounded with interest over 30 years, could be worth $100,000. The 15 minutes you spend negotiating your offer could be the most valuable 15 minutes in your life!
- **You will resent your boss and be more likely to leave your job**. Feeling unappreciated is one of top reasons why employees leave their job. Employees often feel unappreciated when they find out they are underpaid when compared to market rates or their co-workers' compensation. You might blame your boss for making you work so hard for so little. Or you might blame yourself for not asking for what you wanted. Long story short, by not attempting a negotiation, you may resent your boss, your job, and your co-workers for a very long time.

So here is the takeaway: ask for what you want. You deserve it, and employers expect it. Not only will negotiating augment your bank account but also enhance your happiness too.

## Know what you want

This might seem obvious. However, many negotiators have been torpedoed by not knowing what they want. Compensation goals such as "make enough money to retire early" or "spend more time with family" are too vague to be useful in a negotiation. The employer won't know how much "money" will placate you, and you won't know when to stop asking for more.

Use the Negotiation Preparation Worksheet (Resource A in the Appendix) and the Job Offer Comparison Table (Resource C in the Appendix) to think through and clarify what you really want for base salary, signing bonus, vacation time among other issues in the negotiation.

Once you have thought through what you want, define the absolute minimum you are willing to accept. This minimum compensation is known as a reservation price. It is also known informally as the walk away price, and that is the advantage of defining a reservation price: It will help you know when to turn down a deal.

Here is a quick caveat: It is tempting to reveal your reservation price to the other party. Never do that. If you do so, the other party will now target and push for a compensation package that is only slightly above acceptable. In other words, you might leave money on the table if you reveal your reservation price.

## Understand the picture in their heads

Understand the other party's goals. If your argument appeals to the employer's self-interest, your request will resonate with them, increasing odds that they will agree. Stuart Diamond, a negotiation professor at University of Pennsylvania, calls it understanding the picture in the other party's head.

Try to define their negotiation objectives as concretely as possible. In other words, try to find out their reservation price. It will help you determine the maximum the other party is willing to concede and still get an agreement done. In other words, knowing the other party's reservation price will help maximize your compensation.

## Construct the bargaining zone

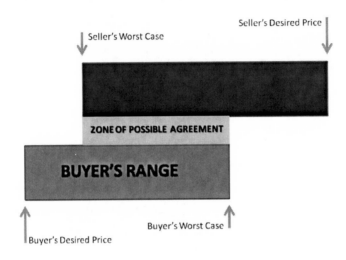

Once you have determined reservation prices, or the worst case scenario, for both parties, the overlap between the worst case scenarios will help you visualize the zone of possible agreement or ZOPA. This term was invented by James Sebenius and David Lax, two Harvard University professors.

During your preparation, the ZOPA can help you determine what your first offer or counteroffer should be. You might want to target a number at the higher end of the ZOPA, knowing that you might inch down from that number with each round of negotiation. Or you might want to target a number just outside of the other party's worst case scenario.

A ZOPA may not exist for two parties. Perhaps the employer cannot afford to pay what the candidate wants. This is common. In that situation, walking away from the offer is preferable to accepting the (undesirable) offer. Do not feel pressured to accept an offer below your reservation price. Doing so is a common regret among candidates.

## Do your research

Information is power, especially in a negotiation. The following pieces of information can help in a negotiation:

- Job levels
- Salary bands
- Company's negotiation philosophy
- Compensation packages at competing companies
- Company's flexibility on each compensation component

Even seemingly minor details, such as how much the company pays the relocation company to move your personal belongings can be helpful. Armed with the information, you can propose substituting that relocation package with an equivalent lump-sum cash payment. Corporate movers are nice, but why pay all that money when renting a U-Haul truck does the job? Hey, hey, hey – it's a U-Haul moving party!

## Have a BATNA

One of the most obvious things you can do to increase your negotiation power is to get a competing offer. Competing offers are frequently linked with a negotiation concept called the Best Alternative to a Negotiated Agreement (BATNA). This term was coined by two Harvard researchers, Roger Fisher and William Ury.

With a competing offer, you will feel more empowered to ask for what you want. If it does not work out with company A, you know you have company B as a backup.

Armed with a competing offer, the employer will also be more willing to give you what you want. You have an option to not take their offer and join the other company. That is a risk they do not want to take. They do not want to lose you; qualified candidates are hard to find!

A BATNA may not always be a competing offer. It could be an option to do something else: start a new business, go to school, or travel the world. As long as your BATNA is a valuable and realistic alternative, you will be more self-assured in asking for what you want. Confidence is critical! Timid and fearful negotiators usually do not have good outcomes.

# The Negotiation

## Set a lofty goal

Psychologists Sidney Siegel and Lawrence Fouraker conducted a landmark study on setting lofty negotiation goals. In the study, the subjects were told to maximize profits in a negotiation simulation. The subjects were then split into two groups. Siegel and Fouraker told one group to achieve $2.10 in profit. Then, they told the other group to achieve $6.10 in profit.

The group with the $6.10 target outperformed the $2.10 group by a whopping 190%. What explains the extraordinary difference between the two groups? The thinking is that those with higher goals are more likely to approach the negotiation differently from those that do not. Specifically, those with lofty goals:

1. Work harder
2. Are more patient
3. Are more assertive

The key takeaway: Always set a lofty negotiation goal.

## Explain what you want

Usually, the other party will help you get what you want if you explain why. Sometimes, explanations make a request more reasonable and acceptable. Other times, explanations provide ammunition that hiring managers can use when explaining your compensation request to their boss.

# Be creative

Negotiation can feel like a battle of wills. That is, two parties are entrenched in opposite positions, and the winner is the one who outlasts the other. I hate to say this, but sometimes the stubborn person wins.

However, that is a win-lose negotiation mentality. Many win-win negotiations arise from creative proposals. Academics call win-win thinking integrative bargaining. That is, after you have taken the time to understand goals, objectives and emotions – from both sides of the table – brainstorm creative ways of reaching an agreement, ideally with the other party.

# Get more information

To come up with more creative proposals, collect more information about the other person's goals. The extra information can inspire both parties to brainstorm and propose new ideas. And creative proposals normally lead to the win-win, integrative scenarios we aspire.

Savvy negotiators collect information from the other party *before* and *during* the negotiation. One tactic to understand the other party's goals during the negotiation is called MESO. MESO stands multiple equivalent simultaneous offers. The idea is to make multiple offers which are equal in your mind. The other party will then react to your multiple offers. Based on their reactions, the other party will reveal their interests, expectations, and preferences. Use this new information to propose new proposals that maximize outcomes for both you and the other party.

# Part 2 Frequently Asked Questions

# Money

## How do recruiters determine fair value for a candidate?

Most recruiters believe what you should make in your next job is linked to what you currently make. We call this approach a market-based approach.

If you are paid above market value then you will have no problem with this approach. However, if you are paid below market value, then you are likely not a fan of this approach.

A candidate who divulges a below-market salary may send an inadvertent but detrimental signal to the hiring manager. Most hiring managers will assume that a poor performance, missing skills, or lack of experience are the reasons for below-market pay. And the hiring manager will be obsessed in trying to figure that out.

Of course, there are non-performance reasons why employees make less than they can get elsewhere. They desire certain projects, want better work life balance, or prefer specific health care packages.

To protect yourself, do not share your current pay during the negotiations. By doing so, you will resist the recruiter's attempts to anchor your future value to your current salary. Instead, defer salary discussions to the end of the interview. And if they push you to reveal a number, it is acceptable to share your expected salary instead. It lets the recruiter know whether the company can afford you without anchoring you to your current pay.

## What is an employer's typical bargaining range?

Most roles have a minimum, mean, and maximum pay rate for a particular job. This is called a salary range or salary band. For many companies, the minimum pay rate is 15 percent less than the mean pay rate. And similarly, the maximum pay is 15 percent greater.

A salary band gives companies flexibility in setting base salary. This flexibility is especially important when a company needs to attract and close candidates from a wide range of work, educational, and geographic backgrounds. Salary bands also give companies the capability to compete for candidates when demand is high and candidate supply is low.

What the salary band concept in mind, if you are a candidate they like, getting a five to ten percent increase should easily be doable. You can assume that you are liked; otherwise, you would not have gotten the offer in the first place.

A higher percentage is doable too, but it will raise eyebrows. You will have to work harder to explain your value.

# Process

## Is it ever bad to negotiate?

Rarely. Unfortunately, many candidates err on the side of not negotiating, fearing that they are not entitled to ask for something that they want. While recruiters and hiring managers may not like negotiating, they fully realize it is an important part of getting talented candidates.

## Do you negotiate salary immediately after the recruiter tells you the number? Or do you wait?

You should wait to negotiate. Instead, focus on getting the offer in writing. We have seen many candidates hastily accepting an offer because they did not get the offer in writing. Feeling desperate after a long job search process, candidates worry that the verbal offer would disappear overnight, if not immediately. Do not make this mistake.

Written offers clearly indicate when they expire whereas verbal offers do not. As a result, verbal offers are more easily rescinded when compared to written ones.

The time it takes a company to prepare a written offer also provides a candidate a moment to reflect. Without reflection, a candidate is more likely to make cognitive decision-making mistakes during a difficult, emotional process.

## Who goes first in a negotiation?

Who should go first in the negotiation? You or the recruiter?

Opinion on this topic is fairly binary: Academics claim that you will have the upper hand if you go first. But the Non-Academics, primarily led by salespeople, claim that it is better to let the recruiter go first.

The truth is that it depends. Sometimes you want to go first; other times, you want to go last. Before we explain, let us explore the discussion from each side of the issue.

## How Non-Academics See the Issue

The Non-Academics argue that you will miss a chance to make more if you go first. Let us say you are making $100,000 per year. You decide to go first. You figure that a 20 percent salary increase is pretty generous. So you blurt out $120,000.

The Non-Academics trigger your sense of regret. What if the other party was willing to pay anywhere from $100,000 on the low-end to $150,000 on the high-end? Asking for $120,000 leaves $30,000 on the table! So the Non-Academics caution you to not make the same mistake again. Next time, you do as they instruct and wait for the recruiter to go first.

## How Academics See the Issue

The Academics argue that the Non-Academics are wrong. The candidate should always go first. Why? You can exploit a psychological quirk called the anchoring and insufficient adjustment bias.

What is anchoring? Anchoring is taking the lead to reveal a piece of information. So in a salary negotiation, that means stating your desired salary first.

What is anchoring bias? It is a psychological bias where individuals make successive judgments based on the first piece of information. So if a candidate tells a Recruiter A that he is worth $200,000, Recruiter A's successive judgment will likely be that this individual is worth at least six-figures. Recruiter A is unable to appropriately adjust away from the initial $200,000 number. This is called the insufficient adjustment bias.

Let us say there is a second recruiter, Recruiter B. Unlike the Recruiter A scenario, the candidate has not revealed the $200,000 asking price with Recruiter B. If a third-party then told recruiter B something outlandish, like the candidate is really worth $50,000, recruiter B is more likely to believe this, not being anchored by the $200,000 asking number.

There is all sorts of interesting studies regarding anchoring bias. One of my favorites comes from Dan Ariely, a professor at Duke University. Ariely found that test subjects bid 60 to 120 percent higher in an auction when they mentally considered a high two digit number vs. a low two digit number, before bidding.

## How We See the Issue

The person with the most information should go first.

Go first if you have researched what the company is willing to pay. For instance, if you know that the most the company is willing to pay is $200,000, then suggest a high number, let us say $220,000. Knowing that the anchoring and insufficient bias will lead the company to settle on a number that is 10 to 20 percent shy of what you suggested. In this case, it would be somewhere between $176,000 and $198,000. From there, you can counter with a value closer to $220,000 such as $210,000. You will likely get another and last counter offer that is close to the $200,000 maximum possible salary.

Do not go first if you have not completed your salary research. You might be surprised at what they will offer you. However, if you do so, you will forgo your ability to use the anchoring and insufficient adjustment bias. The company will be in a position of strength and start the negotiation with a low number. It is unlikely they will start with a high number because the recruiter has done their homework. They know what candidates in your role and industry make. After all, they talk to candidates all day.

## Why does a company ask about competing offers?

There are three main reasons why a company asks a prospective employee about competing offers:

## Assess Your Value

If you are highly valued by others, recruiters, in turn, will also believe that you are valuable too. It is human nature. Other people's opinions validate our beliefs.

So, rightly or wrongly, having competing offers indicates your worth, especially if the offers originate from sought-after companies.

## Speed Up the Recruiting Process

If you are about to accept an offer from another company, your recruiter will put extra effort and emphasis to speed up timelines, especially if you are a desirable candidate.

## Understand the Competition & Give More Attractive Offers

The information helps recruiters identify common competitors and develop more effective strategies to convert those candidates, including more compelling offers.

## Will the company verify my competing offers?

No company would publicly confirm offers they make to candidates.

## The company gave me an offer that's absurdly low. What should I do?

This is a common negotiation tactic called "anchoring." Anchoring is revealing a piece of information with the hope of using cognitive biases to tip the negotiation in the revealer's favor. Once an "anchor" is set, research studies have proven that negotiators use that initial anchor number as a baseline for subsequent haggling. It is difficult in negotiations to move away from the original anchor.

To counteract its effects, cast the anchor off immediately. Label the anchor as too low, and request the negotiating party to immediately make a more realistic offer.

## Is creativity important in negotiation?

One of the keys to negotiation is suggesting creative possibilities. Borrowing a concept from Carol Dweck, a professor from Stanford University, there are people with two different mindsets:

- Fixed mindset: people who believe negotiation opportunities are pre-defined. It is clear what and when you can and cannot negotiate.
- Growth mindset: people who believe negotiation opportunities can be developed. You can create negotiation opportunities yourself.

Dweck maintains how people view themselves contributes to the fixed vs. growth mindset. Those who want to look good (i.e. do not like it when people see them fail) have a fixed mindset. They are less likely to pursue unconventional negotiation strategies (i.e. growth mindset). Those who do not mind not looking cool are more likely to ask for things that others do not think are negotiable.

This is similar to locus of control concept. There are two options: internal vs. external locus. People who have an internal locus believe they have control to change outcomes. They are more likely to be assertive and seek information to improve outcomes. They are also less likely to be vulnerable to feedback. Those with external locus of control feel that life happens to them.

Lesson to be learned: Image is nothing. If you are going to be successful negotiator, you will have to be comfortable being rejected along the way.

## Is it important to understand the other party's objectives?

James Baker once said, "If there was a single key to whatever success I've enjoyed in business and diplomacy, it has been my ability to crawl into the other guy's shoes. When you understand your opponent, you have a better chance of reaching a successful conclusion with him or her. That means paying attention to how he or she views issues and appreciating the constraints they face."

The same applies for salary negotiations: Learn how to empathize with your recruiter or hiring manager. It will make it easier for you to suggest proposals that the other party will accept.

## I get the sense that the hiring manager really likes me, but I'm not getting the job offer. What's going on?

It is likely that your hiring manager is not the sole decision maker. The hiring manager probably needs his or her boss, peers, or other decision makers to approve your job offer.

To close the deal, help the hiring manager make the internal case for your hire. Here are some suggestions:

- Provide the hiring manager content and talking points to explain why you are ideal
- Offer to meet other principals in the decision-making process
- Avoid making statements that will strength the opposition's case against hiring you
- Put external pressure on the other decision makers to make a decision quickly

Academics call this type of negotiation a Level II negotiation. Level I is a traditional negotiation between two parties. Level II focuses on the backroom negotiation necessary to ratify an agreement.

## Why do recruiters roll their eyes when I mention the salary research I've done on Glassdoor, Salary.com, or Payscale.com?

Most recruiters think that online salary data sites are too vague and general to be useful. Salary.com and Payscale.com only take into account the position name. They do not take into account company size, job location, job responsibilities, and most importantly a candidate's skills and experiences.

All of these factors affect one's salary, so it is fair to conclude that online websites are unreliable. Furthermore, some sites such as Glassdoor, use self-reported data, which can be fake.

## Can I negotiate an offer after I've accepted it already?

You can. However, it is bad form to re-negotiate an offer after a candidate has accepted. It gives the impression that the candidate will not uphold their word, hurting trust in the process.

Furthermore, hiring managers hate to deal with candidates who are unsure, difficult to please, or attempting to renege. Hiring managers will get angry and frustrated, thanks to the extra effort and uncertainty the awkward situation will now incur.

Are there times when a candidate should risk a damaged reputation to get more? Possibly. If you are truly dissatisfied with your offer, mature hiring managers understand that it would be better to address it now than later. An unsatisfied employee could put in less than 100% effort on the job, stir discontent among others, or quit their job, leaving the company short-staffed for a period of time.

If you want to re-negotiate, I would recommend that you first acknowledge that re-negotiating is unusual and unprofessional. You will find hiring managers will be more open to re-negotiation if the candidate is apologetic. Go on to explain why you are unhappy with the previously accepted offer. Finally, present your new compensation request.

## How do I get more with a counter offer?

When it comes to renegotiating your salary, here are the top three strategies that come to mind:

## Nibble Strategy

Ever buy a suit? After you commit hundreds or thousands of dollars, the salesperson will ask you to buy ten dollar socks, twenty-five dollar cuff links or a fifty dollar tie. More often than not, the purchaser ends up buying the unnecessary add-on.

Why does this tactic work? In the context of the overall deal, an extra $10, $25 or $50 seems inconsequential.

Try the Nibble Strategy when renegotiating your salary. You have gotten close to the final commitment; ask for a little something extra. It could be an extra $1,000 in base salary, a free gym pass, or three extra vacation days. The counter party will be eager to agree to the inconsequential ask, just so that they can wrap up the negotiation.

## Ratification Strategy

Ever make a decision that makes your spouse angry? Leverage that phenomenon to help you get more money.

That is, tell the other party that you want to accept, but your significant other won't let you. Share what your spouse wants. Collaborate with the company and figure out what counteroffer would make the spouse happy.

This tactic works because every hiring manager, recruiter or decision maker has had a desire, wish or agreement get unwound by his or her spouse in the past.

Why do you think executives ask for fancy motorcycles or sports cars in their compensation package? Their spouse won't let them buy it.

Everyone understands how important to get a spouse's buy-in to close the deal.

## New Information Strategy

New information is a common way to get a party to reconsider an agreement. For a job, it could be a new competing offer. For a house, it could be recent information about toxic waste on the property. For a car, it might be a third-party mechanic who advises replacing the tires or radiator.

If new information changes how one or both parties view the agreement, either party can ask to reevaluate the negotiation.

# Common Mistakes

## I don't like negotiating. Can't I just believe that if I do good work, I'll get the salary I deserve?

Linda Babcock, a Carnegie Mellon professor, points out that job candidates who negotiate earn 7.4 percent more than those who do not ask. Margaret Neale, a Stanford University professor, points out that with the power of compound interest, a $7,000 salary increase, over the course of 30 years, could be worth $100,000.

Salary negotiations are obviously no laughing matter; they could mean the difference of thousands of dollars over your lifetime. However, a Salary.com survey shared that 59 percent of all Americans are afraid of salary negotiations.

So why is that?

- 43% Fear of rejection
- 15% Stingy managers and company
- 15% Would get fired for asking for more money
- 13% Fear other retribution, aside from getting fired, for a raise request gone bad
- 10% Poor company performance
- 4% Bad economy

However, those fears are unfounded. From the other side of the negotiation table, employers report that:

- 73% are not offended when people negotiate
- 84% said they expect candidates to negotiate salary
- 87% reported that they've never rescinded a job offer following negotiations

Companies can be slow in recognizing and rewarding good talent. And with a corporation's desire to maximize the bottom line, managers think: if the candidate is not complaining, why pay more?

Candidates that promote their work and speak up for new opportunities and assignments often find that it is not as difficult as it may seem. Sometimes candidates are shocked by the positive reaction. Not only do they get what they want, but they even find that managers and co-workers are excited about their "sell yourself" efforts. No more mind reading. Your boss now knows exactly what you want.

If this does not feel normal for you, consider finding a negotiation buddy to give you some encouragement!

Reminder: If you want more, just ask.

## Do women negotiate different from men?

Linda Babcock analyzed starting salaries of Carnegie Mellon master's students. Eight times as many males (57 percent) negotiated their salary when compared to females (7 percent). Yes, men appear more likely to speak up for more salary.

Babcock ran another experiment. She informed Carnegie Mellon students that they would be paid between three and ten dollars for playing Boggle, a word game. At the end of the experiment, Babcock handed the subject three dollars and said, "Here's three dollars. Is three okay?" Here is the fascinating finding: nine times as many males asked for more money than females.

Lastly, Babcock found that men negotiate more recently than women. In one Babcock study, on average, the most recent negotiation for men was within the last two weeks. But for women, the most recent negotiation was within the last month.

Interestingly enough, during the study, women were more likely to recall a formal negotiation event such as buying a car or negotiating salary. Men were more likely to recall an informal negotiation event such as conferring with their spouse about who should take kids to soccer practice or asking the boss for a larger rental car on an upcoming business trip due to a recently strained back. In short, men recall negotiation as an ongoing way of life whereas women remember negotiation as a one-time event that does not occur often.

To summarize, women do negotiate differently. They tend to negotiate far less frequently than men do. Academics would argue that societal norms shape the frequency of negotiations for women; that is, perhaps it is not polite for women to ask for something or make a demand. Others would argue that women are more trusting than men that what they currently have is what is fair.

Lesson to be learned: Social norms or not, if you want something, it is okay to ask, early and often.

## I have a verbal offer. Do I need to get it in writing?

One of the most common negotiation mistakes we see is not having an offer in writing. Not getting an offer in writing creates a situation that is fertile for miscommunication and anger.

Imagine this scenario: you enter salary negotiations with Company A. They offer you a low salary, so you reveal an offer from Company B, which has a very attractive compensation package. Company A agrees to match Company B's offer. You now receive $15K more base salary than the original offer. They also include a three percent increase in signing bonus. You are ecstatic and forget to ask for the revised offer in writing. Thinking you got a great deal, you call the other company and reject their offer. A few days later, you get a call from your recruiter. This is what he says:

"I'm sorry but I wasn't able to honor all of our agreed terms for your position. We thought that a $15,000 increase was too much, so we lowered our offer to $9,000. Your bonus will also only be two percent."

You are shocked. How could they take back their offer? You thought it was settled. However, because the offer was not written down, the company believed they were still negotiating with you. After telling you the new terms, the recruiter refused to budge. Now you are stuck with two undesirable outcomes: take the new, less attractive offer or continue to search for a job. With bills to pay, most folks take the offer, unfortunately.

Reminder: Always get the offer in writing.

## I heard I shouldn't share how much I currently make. Is that true?

If there is anything employed candidates could do to reduce the money they get from a job offer, it is divulging what they currently make.

When candidates do this, they are revealing their next best alternative to a new job: their current job. The recruiter's job is to get a candidate to accept without agreeing to an obscene, oversized compensation package.

Armed with a candidate's current salary, then typically offer a five to ten percent premium over what the candidate makes, knowing that the candidate will accept. Most candidates are looking to run from their current job anyway!

Candidates lose out when their share their current salary. The company may have been prepared to give a candidate far beyond a five to ten percent increase. However, knowing a candidate's current salary, there is little incentive for them to beat it.

## Should I tell the employer my absolute bottom line number?

No, you should not tell your employer your absolute bottom line.

Recruiters and hiring managers go into a salary negotiation assuming that you will counter their offer. Reveal your bottom line, and the company's next offer will likely be less than your bottom line. Settling for less is not what you intended.

## Should I use the words "final offer" or anything other phrases that implies an ultimatum?

Avoid any phrase that implies a final demand including last chance, best and final offer, or take-it-or-leave-it.

Ultimatums can destroy trust between two parties because ultimatums project a belligerent, uncompromising negotiation stance. Once trust is lost, it is more difficult to find common ground.

Ultimatums can also put a negotiator in an unusual position. A negotiator can lose integrity if they back down from a previously-labeled final demand.

## I think I rubbed the recruiter the wrong way. What did I do wrong?

How you interact with recruiters will affect how hard they fight for what you want. Here are the top reasons why recruiters get rubbed the wrong way:

### You are arrogant and entitled

Recruiters cannot bear candidates that whine about an offer with a $500,000 base salary. That is a lot of money! Always be humble and respectful.

### You are unrealistic

Recruiters get irritated when candidates have unrealistic compensation expectations. Do your homework. Find out what the market is paying for the job you are pursuing.

### You are hard to appease

If the company made you an offer, most hiring managers will be flexible with the negotiation. They have fallen in love with you. They will ask their recruiter to make the compensation work, so that you will join their team.

But during the negotiation, if you are hard to appease, recruiters are going to be frustrated working with you. They will pass this information to the hiring manager, and you will see both recruiter and hiring manager begin to be less eager and flexible during the negotiation.

## You are begging

Ever hear the following line: "Come on, give me the raise. What is an extra $5,000 a year to your company? You make five billion per year!" Yes, that is begging. Does begging work? Yes. Do recruiters like it? No. They know you are trying to make them feel guilty. Do not try to guilt trip or otherwise manipulate others when trying to get them what you want to do.

## The recruiter doesn't like my counter offer, and she asked me to try again. Is it my turn to make a counter offer, or is it her turn?

It is their turn, not yours. You can try saying, "I just made the last offer. I do not want to bid against myself. What's your offer?"

Do not buckle to the pressure of a tough negotiator. Just like tango, it takes two to negotiate. Unilaterally lowering your requests is not a winning strategy.

## I got an offer from my dream job. I accepted on the spot. What did I do wrong?

There are two problems with accepting an offer on the spot. First, you come across as desperate. The company might also think that they could have gotten you for less money, making you seem like a less valuable candidate. Second, you could be leaving money on the table. By not negotiating, you did not see if the company was willing to pay more.

## I got an offer. I kept pushing for more money. They pulled the offer. What did I do wrong?

Recruiters and hiring managers pull offers from candidates they have fallen out of love with. Here are some reasons why:

- They are getting cold feet about your candidacy.
- They have found another candidate they would like to pursue.
- They have found you difficult during the negotiation process. Maybe you asked for too much. Maybe what you asked for was reasonable, but you asked for it in the wrong way. Team work matters, and you are just not a good person to deal with.

## I got an offer. It was too low. I rejected it immediately. Now I regret it. What did I do wrong?

It seems like you were too emotional and impulsive about the decision. The company didn't even have a chance to remedy your concerns.

Next time, do not react. Instead, pause and consider how you can raise your concerns. Then, improve your offer through negotiation. After exhausting all your options, if the offer is still too low, then you shouldn't feel bad about rejecting it.

# Tactics

## Is it okay to lie or exaggerate offers I do not have?

Trust is an important part of any professional relationship. Any sort of lying, obfuscating, or stammering will not build trust and will damage your relationship.

Not only is lying ethically suspect, but also it is exhausting. It takes extra cognitive energy to keep track of a fabricated story.

## Should I reveal other offers?

Yes.

To get the most amount of money, create value. There are two types of value: intrinsic and extrinsic. Intrinsic value is value you demonstrate during the interview. Extrinsic value is value that is placed on you through external factors, usually outside the interview.

How do candidates build up extrinsic value? Here are two examples:

- Reveal that you are talking to their competitors.
- Disclose offers you have from other firms.

Hiring managers will perceive you as more valuable if you are highly sought after. The greater your value, the more the company will pay to have you on board.

We often hear the excuse: "I do not have any external offers," or "I do not have time or wish to seek employment at competing firms." It is understandable, but as a negotiator, you are missing an opportunity to boost your extrinsic value.

Key takeaway: To get the most amount of value, always start a bidding war.

## The other party thinks I'm being difficult in the negotiation. I'm concerned it's hurting our relationship. How can I relieve the pressure?

In a high-stakes negotiation, your counterparty may be frustrated that you may have a high reservation price. You could be perceived as a stubborn bargainer, intentionally making the situation difficult for him or her.

To relieve that perception and to minimize the hatred, try invoking a higher authority. That is, you cannot accept a lower salary because your spouse would not approve it. The other party will see that you are not intentionally trying to make life difficult for them. Sympathetic to your situation, the company might be more flexible in its own demands.

## I don't want to leave anything on the table. Is it a good idea to get the best possible offer?

Sometimes it is good to give a little to get more.

To elaborate, a personal concession demonstrates how much you want something. A concession also shows your willingness to cooperate towards a common goal, building trust with the other party.

For instance, you might suggest taking a personal loan to pay for relocation costs. The other party may reciprocate by giving you a bigger signing bonus. Going an extra mile, whether it is real or perceived, can work wonders.

## Am I asking for too little?

Many candidates hate to be disappointed, so they set a lower bar to minimize that feeling.

It is not uncommon to set a low bar, especially if a candidate has been out of work for a while. Despite not feeling great about one's job prospects, it is still important to get paid fairly. Do your research and bravely ask for what you are worth.

## Am I asking for too much?

Possibly. If you negotiate and accept an offer that is significantly more than other people at the same level and position, your manager and his peers will hold you to a higher standard. They will expect you to outperform your peers.

Fall short of their now lofty expectations, and you may get poor performance reviews. If layoffs occur, you may be one of the first to go.

## Shorter vesting cycles, tuition reimbursement, sports cars and motorcycles: I didn't know I could ask for these things? Really?

You will never know if you do not ask. Do note that smaller companies are more receptive to creative requests while large companies are less receptive.

Creative requests often fail at large companies not because those companies are not open to imaginative ideas. Instead, large companies struggle to define the appropriate processes and approvers to grant a creative request. In comparison, the approval process at a smaller company is obvious; just ask the CEO.

## What are the best phrases to use when negotiating a salary?

It is amazing how much money you can get when you ask nicely. You can also be amazed what kind of information the recruiter or hiring manager will divulge when you use niceness. Try the following phrases during your next salary negotiation:

- "Is there any wiggle room?"
- "Is there a budget that I should be aware of?"
- "Do you mind if I ask you a question, if it's not too sensitive? What is the salary range for the role?

# What are some different negotiation styles?

David Owens, a management professor at Vanderbilt University, claims that there is a correlation between one's status level and the negotiation tactics they employ. Here is a summary of his findings:

| Individual's Status | Description | Tactics |
| --- | --- | --- |
| High | Disposed to maintain the status quo because they are at the top of the pecking order | Interrupt others, control participation, threaten others |
| Medium | Focus on enhancing their value and importance | Emphasize social capital & expertise, use jargon |
| Low | Focus on social and emotional aspects of the relationship | Beg, eager to volunteer, try to fit in, constantly flatter others |

Low status individuals are more likely to avoid negotiation. They are concerned how asking for what they want will affect their working relationship with the recruiter, hiring manager, or even peers. You will see low status negotiators constantly use flattery and try to please others.

Medium status negotiators typically aspire to be high status individuals. As a result, they are focused on establishing their value and importance. They are most likely to emphasize their skills, experience and their connections. Some people might find medium status individuals to casually mention names of important people (name dropping) or use specialized terms that are difficult for others to understand (jargon). Others may feel medium status individuals claim that they bring more value than they are actually worth.

Unlike medium status negotiators, high status negotiators do not have a need to impress others. They are at the top, and they know it. Instead, they reinforce their status. During negotiation, they are most likely to use threats and control the discussion, especially who gets to participate. They are also very skilled in interrupting others.

# Should I use round or precise numbers when phrasing my negotiation request?

Malia Mason, a professor at Columbia University, ran an interesting study with 130 sets of negotiators. Half the negotiators used a *round number* such as $20,000 for a car negotiation. The other half used a *precise number* such as $21,693 when negotiating for the same car. The result: the precise-number negotiators had an average outcome that was 31 percent better than the round-number negotiators.

What explains this large 31 percent difference? Precise numbers have more credibility. A precise number indicates that the negotiator has done his homework. A precise request is likely based on facts and sound logic.

## Should I negotiate over email?

Despite email's popularity over the last 20 years, we are surprised that there is still debate around whether it is best to conduct negotiation over email vs. phone.

Before we share our conclusions, David Owens, Margaret Neale, and Robert Sutton pose a thoughtful table to explain the differences:

| | Description | Email | Phone |
|---|---|---|---|
| **Completeness** | Message is likely to be detailed and thorough | - | + |
| **Clarity & Feedback** | Opportunity to immediately clarify a message's meaning | - | + |
| **Asynchronous** | Can communicate anytime, without coordinating a time first | + | - |
| **Participation control** | Opportunity for parties to freely share their thoughts | + | - |
| **Immediacy** | Speed of communication | - | + |
| **Emotional display** | Share emotions behind the message | - | + |
| **Permanence** | Written record after the original message has been conveyed | + | - |

Owens, Neale and Sutton also share that:

- Lower status individuals prefer computer-mediated venues, which feel fairer and more egalitarian.
- Higher and medium status folks are also likely to use email. Interestingly, medium status folks are more likely to have longer emails.
- Emails shortcomings, highlighted in the table above, are not as bad as perceived.

Our two cents: email negotiation is acceptable in today's society. Busy professionals and a mobile workforce make it tough to schedule time for two parties to chat. The asynchronous nature of email makes it faster to get things done, and most recruiters and managers realize that. So negotiating by email is absolutely fine.

## What words can I use to deflect questions about my current salary?

We have included phrases you can use to deflect questions about current salary. The phrases will work for both phone and email.

**Variation 1**

"I am uncomfortable sharing my current salary. I do not disclose my personal financial situation to others. I keep that information private."

**Variation 2**

"I signed an NDA with my current employer to not divulge corporate information to others. If you signed a NDA, you wouldn't divulge confidential information to others would you?"

## What words can I use to deflect questions about my expected salary?

We have included phrases you can use to deflect questions about expected salary. The phrases will work for both phone and email.

**Variation 1**

"Why don't we first complete the interview process? If there's a good fit on both sides, I'm sure we can figure out a compensation package that works for both of us."

**Variation 2**

"It's too early to talk about compensation, especially since you don't know the value I can bring to your company. Let's do the interview first, and we can talk about compensation later.

# Raises

## Can I negotiate a raise outside of the normal performance review cycle?

At most companies, it is indeed possible. However, make sure you have a good reason to request a raise outside of a performance review cycle; this would require additional work by your boss, your boss' boss, and the HR department. One good reason is when you have received a competing offer. Another reason is when your position and responsibilities have changed significantly.

# Part 3 Salary Negotiation Scripts for Candidates

# Before Receiving an Offer

## Case 1: What should I do when the online application asks for my salary?

### Story

Jane wants to be a web designer. She's currently working at a company that doesn't appreciate her and her talents, so Jane has been scouring the web to find a new job. Finally, Jane sees an opening at her dream company. She fills out the online application. Everything is going smoothly until it asks for her current and expected base salary.

She's heard that revealing her current salary would reduce her negotiation leverage; it essentially tells her future manager what her best alternative to a negotiated agreement (BATNA) is.

However, the online form won't let her continue if she doesn't divulge it.

What should she do?

### Solution

Jane should list her salary as zero dollars. It has the benefit of not revealing Jane's salary while completing the application. The employer can quickly deduce that Jane is not currently making zero dollars. If the recruiter follows up with Jane about the situation, Jane can explain that she decided not reveal her base salary because it's more important for her to find out if she's a good fit with the company. After the interview process, if it is indeed a good fit, she can tell the recruiter that she's confident that they can find a compensation number that works for both sides.

Jane can also explain her reasoning by emailing the recruiter immediately after she fills out the form.

### Sample Person-to-Person Script

*Recruiter calls Jane on the phone.*

RECRUITER: Hello Jane. We reviewed your application for our new position online, and we are interested in setting up an interview with you.

JANE: That sounds good.

RECRUITER: Before we start talking about the details however, we would like to ask why you wrote $0 for your current salary. Was that a mistake?

JANE: No, it wasn't a mistake. I'm really interested in the position, and money is not a deciding factor for me. I didn't want to state my current salary because I think it is more important for us to figure out if I would be a right fit for the company instead of focusing on the money.

RECRUITER: I see. However, our company policy requires that all candidates enter their current salary information.

JANE: I understand. Why don't we first see whether or not we're a good fit for one another? Then, we can talk about compensation.

RECRUITER: You make a good point. Do you have availability for an interview next week?

JANE: Of course. Let me pull out my calendar and suggest a few times right now.

## Sample Email Script

Dear Recruiter,

My name is Jane, and I applied online for your open position. I'm writing this email as a follow-up to my recently submitted application. In the current and expected base salary sections, there was no option to not divulge, so I wrote $0 instead of my actual and expected salary. I'm really interested in the position, and money is not a deciding factor for me. I didn't want to give my current salary because I think it is more important for us to figure out if I would be a right fit for the company instead of focusing on the money.

I hope that you'll understand my decision. I'm still very excited about the role, and if the feeling is mutual, I'd be eager to discuss this job with you.

Thank you,

Jane

# Case 2: What if the company asks for my current pay stub?

## Story

Before receiving an offer, a Fortune 500 company asked Jane to supply an official, verifiable paystub or W-2 form from her current and past employers. A W-2 form is an official form that reports an employee's wages to the Internal Revenue Service.

Jane is unfamiliar and uncomfortable with this request. Other companies have not requested this in the past. She also feels it's an invasion of her privacy.

Furthermore, asking for paystubs from the last three employers in the last five years is unrealistic. And lastly, shouldn't the company base their compensation offer on what you are worth now, regardless of how much she made in the past?

What should Jane do?

## Solution

### Can a potential employer find out how much an individual makes?

First, a potential employer cannot find out how much an individual makes. In the United States, an individual's salary is considered confidential information. Past and current employers won't divulge or confirm an individual's compensation details. And the government won't release an individual's tax forms without the individual's consent.

*Note: Some entities, especially government organizations, publicly post individual salary data on the Internet. Government organization have adopted this policy to provide transparency to taxpayers, in an effort to curb wasteful spending.*

### Why would a company request paystubs and W-2 forms?

The company is trying to determine a candidate's reservation price. Armed with this information, the company can make an offer that is just enough to persuade the candidate to leave their current employer and join the new company. In other words, by getting candidates to reveal their current salary, companies can pay employees less and save money.

**But why go through the effort of asking for current paystubs? Why not just trust the candidate when they state their current salary during the interview process?**

Most candidates intuitively understand that revealing their current salary reduces their chances of maximize their offer. Lying is one way candidates get around the current salary question.

There are different shades of grey when it comes to lying; it's no different when it comes to the current salary question. Some candidates will be brazen and intentionally inflate their current salary. Other candidates will be coy and confusingly claim their total compensation is their base salary, when it is not.

To sidestep this problem, some recruiters have adopted a new practice: asking for an individual's current paystubs or W-2 form. Once paystubs are in hand, the company can interpret and determine the candidate's true salary.

**Is it illegal for a company to ask for paystubs and W-2 forms?**

No. Companies are free to ask for whatever they want. And candidates are free to divulge as they wish.

**Will I lose the offer?**

Rarely. A recruiter may get a bruised ego when a candidate turns down their request. But do know that good candidates are hard to find. Companies are unlikely to end an individual's candidacy, just because they won't reveal a paystub. This is truer later in the process when the hiring manager is in love with a candidate and on the verge of finalizing an offer.

**So should I share my current paystubs?**

If you have been following our logic, the answer is no. Doing so is tantamount to revealing your reservation price, which increases the chance you'll leave money on the table.

There may be one rare exception. Reveal your current salary only when it is unbelievably high; you feel that it's implausible that the new employer will match. However, you decide to give it a try. Who knows? You might be surprised.

**Should I lie about my salary?**

No. Good negotiators can easily maximize outcomes without lying or bluffing. If a lie gets uncovered, you'll brew mistrust with your soon-to-be employer. It'll also damage your reputation.

**How do I turn down the request?**

To see our suggested approach, read the scripts below.

**Doesn't turning down the request feels confrontational?**

Being assertive helps you achieve sterling outcomes without compromising your ethical values.

And yes, you can be assertive without being nasty or illogical.

## Sample Person-to-Person Script

*Recruiter calls Jane on the phone.*

RECRUITER: Hello Jane. The team enjoyed meeting you last week, and I wanted to collect more details from you.

JANE: I enjoyed meeting the team too. What do you need?

RECRUITER: I need your current paystub.

*Jane hesitates.*

JANE: Why do you need this?

RECRUITER: Oh, it's just something we ask all of candidates. Usually, you can find and print this information from your corporate Intranet.

*Jane takes a deep breath.*

JANE: I apologize, but I am uncomfortable sharing my current salary. I've kept a rule that I do not disclose my personal financial situation to others. That information is private to me.

*Recruiter gets annoyed.*

RECRUITER: I don't see what the problem is. I talked to three candidates this morning, and none of them had concerns with my paystub request.

JANE: I can't speak for them, but I signed an NDA with my current employer to not divulge corporate information to others. If you signed a NDA, you wouldn't divulge confidential information to others would you?

*Recruiter is silent.*

JANE (*breaks the tension*): Are you asking for this information because you're trying to determine my expected salary? If so, I can share my expected salary with you.

RECRUITER: Ok, I'll take that.

JANE: Based on my research for comparable roles and similar sized companies, I am looking for an expected base salary of $200,000.

RECRUITER: Thanks for the information. I'll get back to you soon.

## Sample Email Script

Dear Recruiter,

Thank you for your email. I enjoyed meeting the team last week too.

Regarding your request for my current paystubs, I apologize, but I am uncomfortable sharing my current salary. I've kept a rule that I do not disclose my personal financial situation to others. That information is private to me.

Furthermore, I signed an NDA with my current employer to not divulge corporate information to others. I am uncomfortable with breaking this pledge.

I hope that you'll understand my decision. I'm still very excited about the role, and if it helps, I can share my expected salary. Based on my research for comparable roles and similar sized companies, I am looking for an expected base salary of $200,000.

Thank you,

Jane

## Case 3: What to do if I want to know the budgeted salary range for a job?

### Story

A headhunter from a competitor company contacted Jane for an interview. She's satisfied with her current job and its compensation, but she's curious about the salary range for the new role. She's somewhat interested in the position, but is unsure if the compensation will be close enough to her current salary.

What should Jane do?

### Solution

Jane should politely ask her recruiter what the salary range for the position is. Her recruiter will probably hesitate and not want to reveal the salary range because it will put the company in a weaker negotiating position. The recruiter may also be surprised that the candidate has the audacity to request this information. However, if Jane really feels that she cannot continue the negotiations without salary range information, she should make that clear to the recruiter.

Just so Jane does not appear to be stubborn, she could demonstrate cooperation by offering to reveal her minimum salary requirement afterward. This gesture will make the situation less one-sided. It also shows the recruiter that she's serious about being considered for the role.

### Sample Person-to-Person Script

RECRUITER: Hello Jane. Thanks for agreeing to a follow-up conversation about the position. The company really liked your qualifications and would like you to come in for an interview.

JANE: Thank you! However, I have a question, and I would like to get it answered before I begin interviewing.

RECRUITER: Sure, go ahead.

JANE: If you don't mind me asking, what is the salary range for this role?

RECRUITER: Why do you need to know?

JANE: I have a minimum salary requirement, and if the role doesn't meet it, I don't want to waste your time by interviewing for the position.

RECRUITER: Why don't you tell me your minimum salary requirement?

JANE: I'd be happy to, but I'd like you to answer my question first.

RECRUITER: You seem to be only interested in the salary.

JANE: Of course not. I'm very interested in the role, but I'm afraid the budgeted salary will be too low for my current standard of living.

RECRUITER: I see. Are you sure we cannot continue to the interview to see if you would be a good fit? The company is very interested in you, and the compensation would be quite competitive.

JANE: I would really rather not waste your time.

RECRUITER: You're quite persistent. Alright, the salary range is $104,000-$157,000.

JANE: Great! My minimum requirement is $145,000.

RECRUITER: Perfect. Can we set up an interview time now?

JANE: Of course. Thank you for answering. I'm glad we are on the same page.

## Sample Email Script

Dear Recruiter,

Thank you for reaching out to me about a new career opportunity with your company. I'm very interested in the role, and I'm excited to set up an interview with you. However, I would like to know the salary range for the role before I begin the process. I have a minimum salary requirement, and if the role doesn't meet it, I don't want to waste your time by interviewing for the position. If you also want to know my own minimum salary requirement, I would be happy to reveal it once I get an answer from you.

Thank you,

Jane

## Case 4: What should I do if I don't hear back from the recruiter?

### Story

After Jane was laid off from her job, she desperately searched for a new position. When she saw an open position at a company she really respected, she eagerly applied for the job. Later that day, she received a short screening questionnaire with six follow-up questions including her desired compensation.

Five days after filling out the screening questionnaire, Jane was in a panic. She had not heard back from the recruiter on whether or not she would be called for a phone interview.

"What if they thought that I had asked for too much money?" she thought. Jane assumed the worst and sent the recruiter the following email.

*Dear Recruiter,*

*Perhaps I made you shy away from my application and interest in the system administrator job, as I indicated I wanted to be paid a fair market salary. Perhaps by sharing my experience in receiving similar market salaries in the past, I may have started too high.*

*I hope you noted in my application that I was open and flexible to a variety of compensation arrangements.*

*I hope I gain consideration for the role. I would be an excellent addition.*

*Yours truly,*

*Jane*

Was it the right decision?

### Solution

Jane made the mistake of letting her fears get the best of her.

After not hearing back from the recruiter, she assumed that she made an error by asking for too much money.

There's no evidence to indicate that this was actually the case. Imagine the following alternate possibilities: The recruiter was busy was another project. Or the recruiter was on vacation. In other words, Jane's candidacy was unintentionally put on pause.

By assuming the worst in her email, Jane appears desperate for the job. Desperate candidates are perceived as less valuable, further damaging her candidacy. Finally, Jane also signaled that she could be had for less, even when perhaps the employer was ready to pay more.

In general, no response from a recruiter mean that the recruiter is busy or that the candidate was not qualified. It is quite rare for the recruiter to immediately dismiss a candidate just because of a high listed salary requirement. **If Jane was qualified, the recruiter would normally contact her and ask if her salary requirement was flexible.**

The appropriate email to a recruiter who hasn't responded is to simply ask for a status update, without projecting her fears.

## Sample Person-to-Person Script

*Instead of an email, Jane could have called to check in with the recruiter.*

JANE: Hello, my name is Jane. I recently applied online for the Systems Administrator position.

RECRUITER: Hi Jane, my name is Megan. What can I do for you?

JANE: I just wanted to check in. It's been a few days since I applied, and I wanted to know the status of my application.

RECRUITER: Of course. I apologize for not getting back to you sooner. I was on vacation in Europe and didn't access my work emails. I actually have not yet had a chance to review your application, but I can get back to you within 48 hours.

JANE: That sounds perfect. Thanks for the update.

## Sample Email Script

Dear Recruiter,

My name is Jane, and I recently applied online for the Systems Administrator Position. It has been five days since I filled out the short screening questionnaire, and I have not heard back from your company.

When you get a chance, can you give me a quick update on my application?

Thank you,

Jane

# Case 5: How do I determine my negotiation leverage?

## Story

Jane is wrapping up the interview process with a company. Tomorrow is her last interview. They'll decide shortly after whether or not to give her an offer. She really likes the company and wants to work there.

She's pretty confident that she will receive an offer, but she doesn't know how much leverage she has. Jane knows that having competing offers is her best source of negotiation, but she doesn't have any.

Is there anything else Jane can do to increase her negotiation leverage?

## Solution

Jane should try figuring out how many other people have been interviewing for the position.

If there are plenty of other candidates to choose from, she may not have much leverage in salary negotiations because they can simply choose another qualified candidate. If she is the only real option they have, the company needs Jane and might be willing to give up more money to get her.

There is one caveat: Knowing how many people are vying for the position might not be very helpful. If the company is not in a hurry to fill the position, they might not hire Jane if she is not a good fit. It wouldn't matter if there were many potential employees or if she was the only one.

## Sample Person-to-Person Script

RECRUITER: Hello, Jane. Thank you for taking the time to interview with us. Do you have any questions before we wrap up?

JANE: I do. When do you think I'll hear back from you?

RECRUITER: You'll hear back from us in three weeks.

JANE: Wow, that's later than I thought. Why is your decision process taking so long?

RECRUITER: We have a couple more candidates to evaluate and meet with before we make a decision.

JANE: How many other candidates you are considering?

RECRUITER: We have four other choices. They all have very strong backgrounds. Quite frankly, we could flip a coin and hire any of you. You are all impressively qualified.

JANE: I understand. Thank you for sharing. I really appreciate it.

## Sample Email Script

Dear Recruiter,

Thank you for the interview today. I liked what I heard, and I think I would be a great fit for the company. However, I have a lingering question. How many other candidates are you considering for the position? I am curious how many others are in the running.

If you can't reveal the information, I understand, but I would appreciate it if you could let me know.

Thank you,

Jane

# Negotiating base salary

## Case 6: What should I do to get the salary that others are getting?

### Story

Jane just received an offer for $150,000 at a large multinational company that she really likes. However, her friends, with comparable skills and experience, are getting paid eight percent more at the same company. Jane doesn't think that it's fair to be paid less for the same job, but she doesn't know if her potential employer will feel the same way. She questions whether an appeal for fairness would be effective.

What should Jane do?

### Solution

Progressive companies understand that it's in their favor to pay their employees adequately. Employees that get paid fairly spend more time on their work instead of worrying about what their coworker is making. These employees are also more likely to be loyal and less likely spending their limited time searching for new roles. A lower turnover rate also saves the company time and money looking for replacement employees, along with boosting morale. As a result, most employers want to give their employees adequate pay. So it's worthwhile to appeal to an employer's sense of fairness and ask them to match the salary. Making employees happy is beneficial for both parties.

You can also use Resource B: Comparable Analysis Chart in the Appendix to see how you match up with your friends. You can show the evidence to your boss that you are a comparable match to your friends.

### Sample Person-to-Person Script

JANE: Thank you for the job offer. Your company is my number one choice, so naturally I'm very excited to have received an offer from you.

RECRUITER: You're welcome. Are you ready to accept?

JANE: Not quite. I have heard that others with similar skills and experience have received higher offers. Is that true?

RECRUITER: Well, we don't comment on compensation for other employees.

JANE: My research indicates that that is true, unless you tell me otherwise.

*Recruiter becomes silent.*

JANE: I'd like to negotiate my job offer.

RECRUITER: What did you have in mind?

JANE: I would like to be paid $162,000.

RECRUITER: How did you choose that number?

JANE: Based on my research, that's what other candidates are receiving. I have equivalent skills and experience of those in similar positions, and it's only fair to have the same compensation.

RECRUITER: Okay, we can increase your offer from $150,000 to $162,000.

## Sample Email Script

Dear Recruiter,

Thank you for offering me the position at your company. Your company is my number one choice, so naturally I'm very excited to have received an offer from you.

Before I accept however, I would like to discuss compensation with you. Based on my research, other similar candidates are receiving $12,000 more in compensation. I have equivalent skills and experience of those in similar positions, and it's only fair to have the same salary.

While I would like to work at your company, I can't justify doing so for under the market value. I'm confident that I can add value to your organization, so I hope that we can come to a mutual agreement.

Thank you,

Jane

## Case 7: How do I ask for more salary without upsetting my manager?

### Story

Jane recently received an offer from a top Fortune 500 company. She wanted to negotiate salary, but her hiring manager told her flatly that they "don't negotiate."

Jane is afraid of irritating her future manager. Having a good relationship with her manager is important, but she also wants to be paid fairly.

What should Jane do?

### Solution

Jane's fears are well-founded. Being well-liked is important in the workplace. Negotiators, especially ones that are tough, can be irritable.

However, Salary.com surveyed 1,000 hiring managers and found:

73 percent of employers agreed they are not offended when people negotiate. Furthermore, a whopping 84 percent said they always expect job applicants to negotiate salary during the interview stage. But most importantly, 87 percent said they've never rescinded a job offer following negotiations during the interview, and no employers — that's zero percent — reported demoting or firing an existing employee simply for asking for a raise.

In short, Jane should try to negotiate her salary. But there is a way to negotiate without ruining her relationship with her manager. She just has to be polite and state her case in a professional, respectful manner.

### Sample Person-to-Person Script

JANE: I understand that you said that the salary is non-negotiable, but I would still like to discuss the compensation package with you. I have four years of experience in this industry and an MBA, all things that were preferred but not required of the job applicant. That is why I would like to request a $5,000 increase in your base offer to ensure I'm paid a fair market value.

HIRING MANAGER: I understand your concerns, but the salary is strictly non-negotiable because others in your position are earning the same salary. Giving you a salary increase would cause compensation inequity in our organization.

JANE: I understand. Then could we discuss the other portions of the compensation plan?

HIRING MANAGER: Sure, we could try.

JANE: Instead of the typical yearly review, I would like to revisit my salary in 3 months. This way, I can show you that I am worth that extra $5,000. And since it would be based on merit, it shouldn't stir resentment or create compensation equity problems.

HIRING MANAGER: That sounds fair to me. We would definitely like you on board.

JANE: Great! I'll accept as soon as I get the offer in writing.

## Sample Email Script

Dear Hiring Manager,

Thank you again for offering me the position in your company. I'm passionate about my role, and I'm excited to accept the offer.

However, I would like to request a change in my compensation before I accept. I have four years of experience in this industry and an MBA, all things that were preferred but not required of the job applicant. That is why I would like to request a $5,000 increase in your base offer to ensure I'm paid a fair market value.

I'm confident that this company values its employees and that we can come to a mutually beneficial agreement.

Thank you,

Jane

## Case 8: What should I do if I don't have any competing offers?

### Story

Jane is a 2nd year MBA student at a top school, and she is wrapping up her summer internship at a prestigious company.

Jane's manager is pleased with her performance and prepared to make a full-time offer.

However, the economy is in bad shape, and the employer knows that they are the most desirable company for MBA students. The recruiter tells her that their pay philosophy is to pay at the "65th percentile" and that the company "does not negotiate." They're offering $100,000 base salary. This feels low for top MBA students, who normally receive $130,000 base salary. It's disappointing. However, it is her number one choice.

Jane keeps trying to think of reasons why she should just take the offer as it is. The company is the best fit for her and allows opportunities for fast career growth. She would love to enjoy her final year in business school without worrying about getting a full time job after. She would be thrilled if she didn't have to negotiate because she doesn't think that she is skilled enough to get what she wants.

No matter how hard she tries however, she still can't shake the feeling that she should try to negotiate. She has heard that competing offers would help her increase her negotiation leverage, but she doesn't want to waste time interviewing with companies if she is not interested in working for them.

What does she do?

### Solution

Most MBA students will try to negotiate, but ineffectively. I've seen MBAs commonly ask for a marginal $5,000 increase from $100,000 to $105,000.

By settling for $105,000, the candidate will be disappointed to find out later that the company could have paid up to $125,000 for this level. And given the student's experience, the hiring manager had previously authorized the recruiter to pay up to $120,000. The hiring manager preserved an additional $5,000, on top of the $120,000, for additional negotiation wiggle room.

In addition, for most managers, a ten percent increase in base salary is something managers can readily approve. In this case, the total increase is just five percent.

To negotiate more effectively, the candidate needs to be aware that large, established companies have salary bands. It is usually $\pm$ 15 percent. For most negotiations, like this one, the initial offer is right at the midpoint.

Here is what effective negotiators would do:

- Speculate that the initial offer was at the midpoint
- Guess the salary range for this particular offer
- Counter with a number that was at the top-end or even slightly above the top-end

## Sample Person-to-Person Script

JANE: Thank you for the job offer. I would really like to accept this job, but $100,000 seems low given this position and my prior qualifications.

RECRUITER: Our pay philosophy is to compensate our candidates at the 65th percentile. And unfortunately, we don't negotiate offers.

JANE: Have you paid other MBA interns a higher salary in the past?

RECRUITER: We have, but those individuals bring more work experience to the table.

JANE: If you don't mind me asking, does your company have a salary band for each level?

RECRUITER: Yes.

JANE: And my offer, where does it lie on the salary band?

RECRUITER: I can't really say.

JANE: Is it at the midpoint?

RECRUITER: Yes.

JANE: So is there wiggle room for me to be at the higher end of the salary band?

RECRUITER: Possibly. But I'd have to ask the hiring manager.

JANE: Can you do that for me?

*Recruiter stumbles for a moment*

RECRUITER: Sure, I will ask him for you.

*A few days later, the recruiter arranges a call for the candidate and hiring manager.*

HIRING MANAGER: The recruiter tells me that you're looking for a higher salary.

JANE: Yes, most of my classmates are getting offers at $130,000 base salary. $100,000 seems low relative to that.

HIRING MANAGER: So what are you looking for?

JANE: I would really like to join this company, so I would like to request a $125,000 base salary.

*The hiring manager thinks for a few seconds.*

HIRING MANAGER: I think that's an acceptable number. I can get that in writing for you in a couple of days.

JANE: Great! I look forward to accepting the offer. Thank you again for extending me the position. I know that I will be worth the higher salary.

## Sample Email Script

Dear Hiring Manager,

Thank you for offering me the position at your company. I'm passionate about the role, and I'm excited to start.

Before I accept however, I would like to discuss the compensation package. $100,000 seems low given this position and my qualifications. Most of my classmates are getting offers at $130,000 in base salary with similar positions and qualifications. To get my fair market value, I would like to request being placed at the top end of the salary band for this position. In particular, I would like $25,000 more in base salary to bring my total salary to $125,000.

I would really like to join the company, but it's hard for me to accept when others with comparable skills are making more. I hope you understand, and I look forward to your response.

Thank you,

Jane

## Case 9: What should I do if I almost have a competing offer?

### Story

LinkedIn offered Jane an associate product manager role with a starting salary of $120,000. LinkedIn is Jane's top choice, and she doesn't currently have alternative options.

Jane then finds out that Google is paying $125,000. A friend of hers submitted his resume to Google, but her friend tells her that Google won't accelerate their recruiting process for her, so Jane can't use another offer as leverage.

She wants to accept the LinkedIn offer at $120,000, but would feel a lot better if she could get a higher starting salary of $125,000.

What should she do?

### Solution

A surefire way to increase one's value is to show that other companies are interested in you too.

At the beginning of the interview process, indicate that you are also talking to LinkedIn's top competitor for talent: Google.

You don't necessarily have to have a Google offer. However, indicating that you are being heavily recruited by Google is almost as good as having an actual offer. It shows that you're in demand. The fact that Google is a more desirable employer than LinkedIn makes your threat of passing up LinkedIn more credible.

When you do have an offer with LinkedIn, indicate that while LinkedIn is a top choice, you'd like to wait and see what happens with Google. At some point in your conversation, indicate that Google pays $5,000 more.

The recruiter will likely ask what the company can do to make you choose LinkedIn over Google. Mention your magic salary number whether it's $125,000 or something a little bit more.

The recruiter will then go off and see if the company can fulfill your request. If successful, honor your agreement to accept the LinkedIn offer with the higher base salary.

The recruiter will breathe a sigh of relief, happy to close the deal. And he or she gets to brag about stealing a candidate from Google.

## Sample Person-to-Person Script

JANE: Thank you for offering me the position.

RECRUITER: You're welcome.

JANE: Before I accept however, I would like to discuss the compensation package with you.

RECRUITER: Of course.

JANE: As I mentioned during the interview process, I am still talking to Google about possible positions. While I would prefer to work for LinkedIn, I will have to evaluate Google's offer before I can accept.

*Recruiter listens nervously.*

RECRUITER: I see. Do you have any idea what the compensation will be from Google?

JANE: They have been throwing out $125,000 as a starting base salary. However, if you could match it, I would definitely join your company.

RECRUITER: Sure. We'll increase your base salary to $125,000. I can have that in writing for you in a couple of days.

JANE: That sounds great! I'll be ready to accept once I get the written offer. Thank you for your time and for offering me the position.

## Sample Email Script

Dear Recruiter,

Thank you for offering me the position at LinkedIn. I'm excited about my role, and I'm eager to start.

Before I accept however, I would like to discuss the compensation package with you.

As I mentioned during the interview process, I am still talking to Google about possible positions. While I would prefer to work for LinkedIn, I will have to evaluate Google's offer before I can accept. While I have not yet received a final offer, they have been throwing out $125,000 as a starting base salary. If you could match it, I would definitely join your company.

Thanks for hearing me out, and I look forward to hearing back from you.

Sincerely,

Jane

## Case 10: What should I do if I don't know the market value for a position?

### Story

Jane is interviewing for a software engineering position at Facebook. She's passionate about the company and her industry, but doesn't know how much the average software engineer makes at the company. She knows that she has to do her research before entering into salary negotiations, but doesn't know where to find accurate information.

What can she do?

### Solution

One under-utilized resource for salary data in the U.S. is the H-1B data collected by the United States Department of Labor. It is a collection of companies, salaries, and positions paid to foreign employees with specialized skills who come to work in the United States. Companies who employ people that fall under the H-1B classification must reveal salary data for those positions. While the H-1B classification does not apply to everyone, the salary data can be a great resource for those looking for salary data for a particular company and position.

Here is how to access the data.

1. Access this website:
   http://www.foreignlaborcert.doleta.gov/performancedata.cfm
2. Click on the "Disclosure Data" tab.

3. Scroll down to find the first table and download the H-1B File.

| OFLC Program | FY 2014 Disclosure File | File Structure |
|---|---|---|
| PERM | PERM_FY2014_Q3.xlsx | PERM_FY14_Record_Layout.doc |
| H-2A | H-2A_FY14_Q3.xlsx | H2A_FY14_Record_Layout.doc |
| H-2B | H-2B_FY14_Q3.xls | H2B_FY14_Record_Layout.doc |
| LCA | H1B_FY2014_Q3.xls | H1B_FY14_Record_Layout.doc |
| Prevailing Wage | PWD_FY14_Q3.xlsx | PWD_FY14_Record_Layout.doc |

4. Locate the information you want.

   a. Positions are listed under the column called "LCA_CASE_JOB_TITLE".

   b. Employers are listed under the column called "LCA_CASE_EMPLOYER_NAME".

   c. Compensation is listed under the column called "LCA_CASE_WAGE_RATE_FROM".

   d. The "LCA_CASE_WAGE_UNIT" reveals if the compensation is an hourly or yearly wage.

Now Jane can search for a person who works for Facebook and is a Software Engineer. In Fiscal Year 2014, the range of software engineers at Facebook is around $100,000-$200,000 with an average of around $140,000.

## Sample Person-to-Person Script

JANE: Thank you for offering me the software engineering position at Facebook.

HIRING MANAGER: You're welcome.

JANE: Before I accept however, I would like to discuss the compensation. The base salary of $108,000 is too low for my experience and qualifications. Facebook seems to pay its entry level software engineers at the bottom of the pay level at $100,000, only $8,000 less than what you are offering. However, I have six years of programming experience from Apple.

HIRING MANAGER: I see. So what salary are you suggesting?

JANE: I think that I should get paid in the middle range at $140,000.

HIRING MANAGER: Where are you getting your information?

JANE: I got it from the U.S. Department of Labor website.

HIRING MANAGER: I see. Would you be willing to accept $135,000? $140,000 is out of the budget.

JANE: How about $139,000?

*Hiring manager flashes a grin*

HIRING MANAGER: You don't miss much do you? Sure, $139,000 works.

JANE: Perfect. I accept. I'm looking forward to being part of the team.

## Sample Email Script

Dear Hiring Manager,

Thank you for offering me the software engineering position at Facebook. I'm excited to accept and begin contributing to the company.

Before I accept however, I would like to discuss the compensation. The base salary of $108,000 is too low for my experience and qualifications. Facebook seems to pay its entry level software engineers at the bottom of the pay level at $100,000, only $8,000 less than what you are offering. However, I have gained six years of programming experience at Microsoft, an equally prestigious company. According to the U.S. Department of Labor, I should get paid in the middle range at $140,000.

I'm confident that I can add a lot of value to Facebook and I hope that we can come to a mutual agreement.

Thank you,

Jane

## Case 11: What do I do if the recruiter won't accept my salary research?

### Story

Nike just offered Jane an entry level position in their sales department. When Jane reviewed their compensation package, she was disappointed. The offer seemed low, so Jane went to do some research on her market value in that position. According to online sources such as Salary.com and Payscale.com, Jane should have been receiving $9,000 more.

When Jane explained her research to the recruiter however, the recruiter dismissed it. The recruiter claimed that those online sources were not accurate enough to be taken seriously in a negotiation. Jane was dumbfounded. She didn't know how to continue the conversation. Missing a counter reply, Jane accepted the job offer although it was low.

What should Jane have done?

### Solution

There are two other options that Jane could have taken: identify new sources of salary data or reject the low offer.

**New Sources of Salary Data**

It's important to support your salary request with a credible reason. The best explanation for an increased salary is another job offer. Multiple offers attests how much others are willing to pay you. The more lucrative the competing job offer, the more the company wants you to join. The other offer is also a credible threat that you may turn down the company in question.

The second best piece of evidence that Jane could have used is personal contacts within Nike who can definitively say how much employees in a certain position are earning.

The third best piece of evidence Jane could have leveraged is the anticipation of a competing offer. If the competitor was talking about a larger salary, it could prompt Nike to offer a higher salary even if Jane hadn't formally received another offer.

### Reject the Offer

The second option is rejecting the low offer. Because Jane was caught off guard, she made a rash decision and accepted the offer. If she had thought more carefully about the situation, she might have rejected the offer and explored other companies. She might have found a position in a company that pays fairly.

## Sample Person-to-Person Script

### Option 1

JANE: Thank you for your offer. I'm very excited about working for Nike. Before I accept, I would like to discuss the compensation package.

RECRUITER: Of course. What did you want to talk about?

JANE: I believe I'm being underpaid for this position and my skills. According to my contacts in Nike, I should be making about $9,000 more in base salary.

RECRUITER: That's interesting. Which position does your contact hold?

JANE: She is a marketing manager in the Beijing office. Due to the differences in cost of living from here and Beijing, she calculated how much her average employee salary would be at Beaverton, Oregon. She found that it should be about $9,000 more than what you offered.

RECRUITER: I see. Alright, I think that we can add an extra $9,000 to your base salary. Of course, I would have to get the new base salary approved by my supervisor. Anything else?

JANE: I don't have anything else to add. Thank you for your help and offering me the position. I'm ready to accept once the base salary gets approved, and I get it in writing.

**Option 2**

JANE: Thank you for your offer. I'm very excited about working for Nike. Before I accept, I would like to discuss the compensation package.

RECRUITER: Of course. What did you want to talk about?

JANE: I believe I'm being underpaid for this position and my skills. According to salary websites, I should be making about $9,000 more in base salary.

*Recruiter rolls her eyes.*

RECRUITER: Online salary calculators are often inaccurate. They don't factor in the position details, your experience and skills, the job location and other compensation package details. I'm sorry. I can't accept your online salary research.

*Jane shifts uncomfortably. She's dumbfounded and doesn't know what to say.*

RECRUITER: Our offer is firm. The compensation is very competitive, so I can't increase the salary for you.

JANE: I see. Well I would still like some time to evaluate the offer. When do you need a decision?

RECRUITER: By the end of next week.

JANE: Great. I'm sure I'll have an answer for you much earlier than that. Thank you for offering me the position, and I look forward to speaking again.

## Sample Email Script

Dear Recruiter,

Thank you for your offer. I'm excited to begin working for Nike.

Before I accept, I would like to discuss the compensation package. I believe I'm being underpaid for this position and my skills. According to my contact in Nike, I should be making about $9,000 more in base salary. My contact is a sales manager in the New York office. Due to the differences in cost of living from here and New York, she calculated how much her average employee salary would be at this branch. She found that it should be about $9,000 more than what you offered.

I'm eager to begin working for Nike, and I'm confident that I can bring a lot of value to the company, but I cannot accept a below market position. I hope that we can come to a mutual agreement.

Thank you,

Jane

## Case 12: What should I do if I need more money for gas?

### Story

Jane would like to ask for a $3,000 base salary increase before accepting a new job offer. However, the company won't budge. She wants the additional cash to cover the extra expense of a longer commute. However, she has not mentioned that reason to the company during her negotiations.

What should Jane do?

### Solution

To get what you want, include your justification. A Harvard psychologist, Ellen Langer, found that strangers are more likely to agree to a request when you explain why.

In Langer's experiment, researchers asked the control group, "Excuse me, I have five pages, may I use your Xerox machine?" 60 percent said yes. However, researchers asked the experimental group a slightly different question, "Excuse me, I have five pages. May I use the Xerox machine because I have to make some copies?" 93 percent said yes. By including justification, the acceptance rate increased 33 percent.

### Sample Person-to-Person Script

JANE: I would like to discuss my compensation with you again.

HIRING MANAGER: We already talked about a lot of things about your compensation, didn't we?

JANE: Yes we did, but I wanted to clarify something that we didn't reach an agreement about. I mentioned that I would like an extra $3,000 in base salary. I'd like to get that extra $3,000 increase because my commute will increase an additional 25 miles from Ontario to Westwood. I'm assuming that gas is $4 a gallon, which would be an extra $2,000 after tax. Factoring a 33 percent tax rate, $3,000 is a reasonable increase.

HIRING MANAGER: I'm glad you explained why you wanted more money. That seems like a reasonable request, and I believe we can approve your salary request.

JANE: Thank you. I'm excited to start working at the company. I'll be ready to accept the offer once I get it in writing.

## Sample Email Script

Dear Hiring Manager,

I would like to discuss my compensation with you again. I mentioned earlier that I wanted an extra $3,000 in base salary, but I didn't explain why, so I would like to do that now. I'd like to get that extra $3,000 increase because my commute will increase an additional 25 miles from Ontario to Westwood. I'm assuming that gas is $4 a gallon, which would be an extra $2,000 after tax. Factoring a 33 percent tax rate, $3,000 is a reasonable increase from $2,000.

That would raise the initial offer from $130,000 to $133,000. I'm very interested in the role, and I'm confident that I can bring a lot of value to the company. I hope we can reach a mutual agreement.

Thank you,

Jane

## Case 13: What should I do when my new offer is less than my current salary?

### Story

Jane has been working at her current company for four years as a software developer. A headhunter recently contacted her and asked her to interview at a competitor. She is interested in the competitor because she'll be working on a top secret mobile app project.

The interview was a great success, and the hiring manager made Jane an offer. However, the new offer was $15,000 lower than her current salary.

What should Jane do?

### Solution

Jane can use her current salary as leverage. By revealing what she currently makes, Jane can explain that it doesn't make sense for her to join the new company and make less.

A current position can be used in the same way as a competing offer. If the new company really wants you, they will have to give you a better offer.

### Sample Person-to-Person Script

JANE: Thank you for offering me the position in the mobile department. However, I'm not sure if I am willing to switch positions.

RECRUITER: I see. Was our offer not attractive enough?

JANE: Well, yes. The salary is much lower than what I currently make.

RECRUITER: How much is that?

JANE: My current salary is $15,000 more than your offer.

RECRUITER: I see. Have you looked at the full compensation package?

JANE: Yes I did. When comparing both compensation packages, my current one is far superior.

RECRUITER: Would you be willing to accept the new position if we matched your current salary?

JANE: Absolutely. I'm ready for a change, but I can't justify leaving my current job for a job that pays significantly less.

RECRUITER: Then I'll see what I can do. I know the team loved you and that you're a great fit for the company, so I'm sure that we can come to an agreement.

JANE: Thank you very much. I am excited to hear back from you.

## Sample Email Script

Dear Recruiter,

Thank you for offering me the position in the mobile department. However, I'm not sure if I am willing to switch positions. The salary is much lower than what I currently make. In fact, my current salary is $15,000 more than your offer.

I also looked at both compensation packages, and my current benefits package is more attractive. However, I am very interested in the new role. I'm willing to accept the new position if the company could match my current salary. I'm ready for a change, but I can't justify leaving my current job for one that pays significantly less.

I'm confident that I can add a lot of value to the company. I hope that we can come to a mutual agreement.

Thank you,

Jane

# Case 14: I don't know what I want. I just want more. How should I negotiate?

## Story

Jane received four offers from different companies. There's one company, Baxter, that was clearly her favorite, but the offer was very low. Jane wants more money, but doesn't know how much.

Jane explains the situation to her friends. They tell her being vague isn't helping. Her friends tell her that she has to be clearer about what is an acceptable offer.

Rather than raise the offer, the recruiter and hiring manager are busy telling her why she has misunderstood their offer. They keep explaining to her that their offer is superior, but Jane refuses to sign. It's not clear if she ignores their reasoning or if she's not sure what to do next.

The recruiter and hiring manager also start prying into the other offers. Jane is vague about the competing offers. Jane is also getting frustrated with the invasion of privacy, and they're frustrated with her stonewalling.

Jane doesn't see it that way. She's just frustrated that her number one choice isn't giving her a better offer. But she doesn't want to accept her number two choice either.

What should Jane do?

## Solution

Jane should decide exactly what she wants and clearly advocate for her interests. She is expecting the recruiter and the hiring manager to fight on her behalf and arbitrarily increase the offer, but they have no incentive to negotiate against themselves.

Even though she thinks it is an invasion of privacy, Jane also has to reveal some aspects of her other offers if she wants to use them as leverage. With only vague hints at other offers, the recruiter and hiring manager do not know if the offers are real and serious. Jane should show how much the other companies value her and explain why the other offers are more attractive. Without that information, Baxter may not know how low Baxter's offer really is.

## Sample Person-to-Person Script

JANE: I think that I might have been going about this negotiation the wrong way. I have been very indecisive about what I wanted out of the job offer, and I think it might be causing unnecessary tension. I want to emphasize that I wasn't intentionally stalling or being difficult, but I was not sure what I wanted. After much thought, I decided what I needed from the job offer.

HIRING MANAGER: That is good to hear. We were worried you were stonewalling.

JANE: I apologize for doing that; that's my mistake.

HIRING MANAGER: We appreciate that. Shall we proceed?

JANE: Absolutely. To start, I would like a $17K increase in my base salary. I have offers from two other companies that are offering an extra $20K in base salary.

HIRING MANAGER: Our base salary might be a little low, but as we said before, we have a very generous benefits package.

JANE: Actually, your benefits package is not as attractive as some of the other companies. In fact, most of them had a few more vacation days, a company laptop or phone, or more stock options.

HIRING MANAGER: I see. How can we reach an agreement then?

JANE: My second choice company, in addition to $20K more in base salary, also includes a company car with gas, insurance, and maintenance costs covered. However, instead of a company car, I would like five extra paid vacation days and a gas allowance of $3,500 to cover the fuel expense of driving to work.

HIRING MANAGER: It's great that you're being very specific. We can approve your request of the extra vacation and the gas allowance.

JANE: Great! I can accept once I get the revised offer in writing. I'm relieved we could reach an agreement.

HIRING MANAGER: We're glad that we could come to a mutual agreement as well. We'll send you that written offer in a few days.

## Sample Email Script

Dear Hiring Manager,

I would like to discuss my compensation with you again because the last conversation did not end very well. I think that I might have been going about this negotiation the wrong way. I have been very indecisive about what I wanted out of the job offer, and I think it might be causing unnecessary tension. That's my mistake, and I apologize. After much thought, I figured out what I needed from the job offer.

To start, I would like a $17K increase in my base salary. Two other companies that I received offers from are offering $20K more than your compensation offer.

My second choice company, in addition to $20K more in base salary, also includes a company car with gas, insurance, and maintenance costs covered. However, instead of a company car, I would also like five extra paid vacation days and a gas allowance of $3,500 to cover the fuel expense of driving to work.

I'm trying my best to be clearer about what I want. I hope this makes the negotiation more straightforward from here on out. I'm confident that I'm a good fit for you company, and I hope we reach an agreement soon.

Thank you,

Jane

## Case 15: How do I determine if I have any negotiation leverage?

### Story

Apple just made an offer to Jane to join as the marketing director. The offer is $175,000, a little low for a marketing director at Apple. However, Apple is releasing a new product soon and needs a new director ASAP, so the hiring manager is under pressure to fill this role quickly.

What should Jane do?

### Solution

The key here is to understand your negotiation leverage. What are their alternatives? In other words, if the hiring manager can't make the deadline, what will Apple do? Jane needs to find out if their alternative is better than paying Jane more money.

### Sample Person-to-Person Script

JANE: Thank you for the job offer. I have a few questions.

HIRING MANAGER: Sure, go for it.

JANE: For the first 30 days, where would you like me to focus on my attention?

HIRING MANAGER: We're launching a new Apple iRefrigerator, and I'd like you to head up our marketing effort.

JANE: Who do you have working on it now?

HIRING MANAGER: We have a talented senior marketing manager heading up that effort. She's a fantastic operator. Projects are delivered on-time, and she works well with others. However, she doesn't have the stature or gravitas to represent us at external events, such as keynote speeches, press events, and partnership discussions.

JANE: Who would do this if I didn't come on board?

HIRING MANAGER: It would fall on my plate, but honestly, I don't have the time to take care of this now, especially since there's another big product launch, the new Apple iDryer, that I'm working on.

*Jane calls the hiring manager back two days later*

JANE: Is there wiggle room in the base salary?

HIRING MANAGER: What did you have in mind?

JANE: I'm asking for $240,000.

HIRING MANAGER: How did you come up with that number?

JANE: There are three main reasons. First, I have over 15 years of experience representing high tech firms at press events for new product launches. I've done demos at SXSW, Google I/O and Build, among others. Second, I have experience with not only successful product launches but controversial ones as well. I represented Google for the Gmail launch. While many early adopters loved it, it raised some privacy concerns. I was on the front-lines – managing consumer perception and representing the company when the California legislature proposed a bill to shutdown Gmail for scanning user emails. Lastly, I have in-depth relationships with several top executives in the industry spanning both software, such as Google and Microsoft, as well as hardware such as Samsung, HP and Dell.

HIRING MANAGER: You do make a good point, and that's why we made you this offer. You have some unique skillsets. $240k is a bit rich though. Can you do $220k?

JANE: If you can do $230k, we have a deal.

HIRING MANAGER: Done.

## Sample Email Script

Dear Hiring Manager,

Thank you for offering me the Marketing Director role at Apple. I'm very passionate about the company and the position.

Before I accept however, I would like to discuss my compensation package with you. More specifically, I would like to request a base salary increase to bring my salary to $240,000.

I have three main reasons for requesting this number. First, I have over 15 years of experience representing high tech firms at press events for new product launches. I've done demos at SXSW, Google I/O and Build, among others. Second, I have experience with not only successful product launches but controversial ones as well. I represented Google for the Gmail launch. While many early adopters loved it, it raised some privacy concerns. I was on the front-lines – managing consumer perception and representing the company when the California legislature proposed a bill to shutdown Gmail for scanning user emails. Lastly, I have in-depth relationships with several of the top executives in the industry spanning both software, such as Microsoft and Google, as well as hardware such as Samsung and LG.

As you can see, I have much more experience than your average Marketing Director, so I believe my value is above $175,000.

I'm confident that I can bring a lot of value to the marketing department and to Apple overall, so I hope that we can come to an agreement.

Thank you,

Jane

## Case 16: What should I do if the hiring manager won't budge on compensation and stalls the negotiation?

### Story

Jane received a job offer at a new company and wants to negotiate. When she arrives at the negotiation table, the hiring manager is very stubborn. The hiring manager doesn't budge on any of the issues.

What should Jane do?

### Solution

In a stalled negotiation, Jane can use a technique called logrolling. Logrolling is the practice of exchanging favors to reach a goal. It's often used in a political context where one politician will agree to vote for a proposed bill as long as the other party agrees to do the same for a different bill. They are both doing a small favor in exchange for something that they care about.

### Sample Person-to-Person Script

JANE: I feel like we cannot seem to agree on any part of the compensation package. Perhaps we could prioritize to make sure that we both get what is important to us. So, which of these things really matter to the company?

HIRING MANAGER: All of them matter to the company.

JANE: Well, wait a minute. They can't all be of the same importance. Which ones are the most important?

HIRING MANAGER: It's not my job to prioritize...It is my job to deliver what my colleagues have asked for.

JANE: I don't see how this negotiation can move on without prioritizing the terms of the compensation package. I can't accept this package as it is, so we're going to have to work together to find a mutually beneficial agreement.

HIRING MANAGER: Alright then. Why don't you make a proposal first?

JANE: Okay. I would like to increase my salary by $7,000. I'm willing to give up the company phone.

HIRING MANAGER: We're willing to increase your salary if you will also give up $10,000 of your signing bonus.

JANE: I can accept that if you will give me four more vacation days.

HIRING MANAGER: That sounds fair. We'll increase your salary by $7,000 and four more vacation days. You will give up the company phone and $10,000 of your signing bonus. Does that sound right?

JANE: Yes. Thank you for your time. I'll be ready to accept once I receive the full offer in writing.

## Sample Email Script

Dear Hiring Manager,

Thanks for taking the time to chat with me yesterday. Here's what I understood from our conversation yesterday:

- You've presented me with your best and final offer.
- You have strong candidates in the pipeline, and you'll make an offer to your number two candidate if I decide not to take it.
- You don't like it when candidates negotiate offers.

I appreciate your willingness to hear my concerns, and I agree that negotiation is not a pleasant experience.

However, I do take my career seriously, and once I commit to a company, I intend to be with the company for a very long time. As uncomfortable as negotiation may be, I'm not comfortable accepting your offer as-is. I have other offers on the table that have compensation packages that are more in-line with my priorities, and it's hard for me to pass up on those offers and accept one that's less competitive.

To show my willingness to work with you, I am willing to sacrifice the company phone and signing bonus. My top priorities are base salary and vacation days. I'm prepared to brainstorm with you different tradeoffs to see what would best work for you.

Let me know when you're ready, and we can schedule time to discuss.

Sincerely,


Jane

## Case 17: What should I do if I get a ridiculously low offer?

### Story

Jane's dream company just made her an offer, and it's for $40,000. She is shocked that it's so low. The market rate for this position is $120,000, and friends in similar roles make $150,000.

Setting aside the abysmally low salary, this company would be her number one choice.

What should Jane do?

### Solution

This is a common negotiation tactic. Most people call it "low balling" while academics call it "anchoring." Anchoring is revealing a piece of information with the hope of using cognitive biases to tip the negotiation in the revealer's favor. Once an "anchor" is set, research studies have proven that negotiators use that initial anchor number as a baseline for subsequent haggling.

In this case, the initial $40,000 is a low ball offer. The recruiter is expecting you to suggest a high number, but your subsequent number whether it's a 50 percent or a 100 percent increase is only $60,000 or $80,000, which is still lower than the market rate of $120,000.

Jane's solution here is to not dwell on this anchor. Instead, re-establish the negotiation with her own anchor point.

### Sample Person-to-Person Script

RECRUITER: We'd like to make you an offer with a base salary $40,000.

JANE: Thanks for the offer, but I was wondering: "How did you come up with that number?"

RECRUITER: That's based off of salary data that we have along with the standard offer we give to all of our software engineering candidates.

JANE: That's much lower than I expected. My market research actually indicates that I should be making $150,000.

RECRUITER: Perhaps I didn't clarify that the $40,000 is just the base salary. Let me walk you through the total compensation. It includes stock options, full medical benefits, free lunch and dinner...

JANE: I appreciate you walking through the offer, but I just cannot accept $40,000. My counteroffer is $150,000 for base salary.

RECRUITER: Did you notice that our offer includes a transportation benefit too? You can either get a free bus pass or a free mountain bike worth up to $500.

JANE: I really appreciate the offer, but if you cannot do closer to $150,000 then I will have to end the discussion.

RECRUITER: I see. How about $120,000 for base salary?

JANE: How about $130k?

RECRUITER: I can do $125k.

JANE: I'll agree to that. Can you send me the updated written offer?

RECRUITER: It'll be in your inbox by the end of the day.

## Sample Email Script

Dear Recruiter,

Thank you for offering me the position at your company. I'm excited about the role, and I'm eager to join.

However, I would like to discuss my compensation package with you.

My market research indicates that a fair salary for this position would at least be $120,000. With my qualifications, my market value would be closer to $150,000. While I am excited about this position, I cannot accept an offer as low as $40,000. I'm confident that I can bring a lot of value to the company, so I hope that we can come to a mutual agreement.

Thank you,

Jane

## Case 18: What should I do if the salary is too low for the position but way more than what I currently make?

### Story

Jane is a journalist at a medium-sized newspaper company. While she's at lunch, her phone alerts her to a new email. When she opens it, Jane can't believe her eyes. She's looking at an offer letter from a large corporation asking her to be their new PR Director. Her shocked face grabs the attention of her friend and coworker, Megan. Megan looks over the letter and her jaw drops too.

"That's so much money!" she exclaims. "It's vastly more than what you're making now."

Jane looks incredulously at Megan. "Yes, it's more than a journalist's salary," says Jane. "But it's extremely low for a PR Director!"

Jane feels insulted. She's excited that they offered her the position, but finds it unfair that they pay her so little.

What should she do?

### Solution

Your salary at a new job should not hinge on what you made in your last job. Even though the offered salary is much higher than Jane's current salary, she should be paid fairly for the work she does. Since she is going to fully take on the PR Director role, she should be compensated in full as well. Jane should definitely attempt to negotiate the offer.

### Sample Person-to-Person Script

JANE: I will be underpaid for this role if I accept it. The market rate for a PR Director is 20 percent higher.

HIRING MANAGER: That's true, but you would be a brand new PR director with no experience.

JANE: Well, none of the other PR directors have the contacts that I have from my journalism days.

HIRING MANAGER: Hmm, that is true.

JANE: I really appreciate the offer, but it's not fair for me to accept a below market salary when I bring expertise and connections that others don't have. Regardless of my previous job history, I should get a salary appropriate for the position.

HIRING MANAGER: You make a good point. Let me think about it and get back to you.

## Sample Email Script

Dear Hiring Manager,

Thank you for offering me the PR Director position. I'm excited to take on a new role at this company.

However, I would like to discuss the compensation. If I accept now, I will be underpaid for this role. The market rate for a PR Director is 20 percent higher than your current offer. While I do not have experience as a PR Director, I do have contacts and connections from my years in the journalism industry to bring to the table.

I really appreciate the offer, but it's not fair for me to accept a below market salary when I bring expertise and connections that others don't have. Regardless of my previous job history, I should get a salary appropriate for the position.

I hope you can approve my request for a 20 percent increase in my base salary. I'm confident that I can bring a lot of value to the company.

Thank you,

Jane

# Case 19: What should I do if I'm getting emotional over a decision?

## Story

After a long job search, Jane's effort paid off. She received four offers from different companies. Pinterest clearly stood out as her favorite company.

Pinterest's team and managers were super smart, but exuded the boy and girl next door charm. The company's core product was strong, and their recent forays into adjacent verticals seemed very promising. Lastly, this was Jane's chance to get equity for an early-stage startup.

There was one big problem however: this company's offer wasn't as attractive as the 2nd best option.

The 2nd best option was offering six times more in stock grants, $25k more in base salary, and $20k more in annual bonuses.

Jane knows that she shouldn't be emotional about the decision, but she liked Pinterest so much that she was willing to forgo additional compensation. But Jane couldn't shake the nagging feeling that she was leaving moving on the table.

What should Jane do?

## Solution

Jane should still try to negotiate with Pinterest by leveraging her other job offer. Even if they can't fully match the other company's compensation, they can probably give her more money or equity. Jane is really confident in the future success of the startup, so in the long run, Jane might actually make more money than the short-term gains of a higher salary at the second company.

Jane also needs to consider the non-monetary benefits of working at Pinterest. She is passionate about the product, likes her coworkers and managers, and loves the company culture. Jane initially believed that these intangible benefits were worth more than the extra money. However, when she thought more rationally, she wasn't sure. To make an informed decision, Jane needs to decide logically if these benefits are worth more than the larger salary and equity she would get at the other company. If these intangible benefits alone aren't enough to fully persuade Jane, she can also ask for other non-monetary benefits such as a better job title, more vacation time, or an earlier review date.

## Sample Person-to-Person Script

JANE: Thank you for offering me a position at Pinterest. I'm excited about the company and the position, but I would like to discuss compensation. I understand that you are a startup and that money is tight, but I have received another job offer that is more attractive than Pinterest's. In fact, they are offering six times more in stock grants, $25K more in bonuses, and $20K more in base salary.

HIRING MANAGER: Wow. That is a lot. Unfortunately, Pinterest we cannot match that offer, but I would be happy to discuss ways we can bridge the gap, if you are interested.

JANE: Of course I am. I'm looking for at least $8,000 more in base salary. Could that part be revised?

HIRING MANAGER: We can do $8,000, but not more than that.

JANE: I see. Then can we discuss non-monetary benefits?

HIRING MANAGER: What did you have in mind?

JANE: I would like an extra week of paid vacation and a six month early review.

HIRING MANAGER: We can do the extra week of vacation but I will have to talk to the HR director about the early review. If that is possible, will you accept the offer?

JANE: Yes, I will. Please let me know what she says.

## Sample Email Script

Dear Hiring Manager,

Thank you for offering me a position at Pinterest. I'm excited about the company and the position, but I would like to discuss compensation. I understand that you are a startup and that money is tight, but I have received another job offer that is much more attractive than Pinterest's. In fact, they are offering six times more in stock grants, $25K more in bonuses, and $20K more in base salary.

I understand that Pinterest is a startup and can't offer the same kind of pay, so I'm willing to be flexible because I really like the position. That is why I would like to ask for only $8,000 more in base salary and an extra week of paid vacation and a six month early review.

I don't expect Pinterest to match the competing offer, but if these portions of the offer can be revised, I would be happy to accept.

Thank you,

Jane

# Negotiating a bonus

## Case 20: What should I do if I'll lose my annual bonus by joining a new company?

### Story

Jane just received a new job offer at a successful company. They want her to start on November 1st, but Jane will lose her year-end bonus if she leaves before December 15th. Jane asked if they could move the start date to the end of December, but her new company says that they need her now for a critical project. She wants to change jobs soon because she is really passionate about the new position, but she doesn't want to forgo her $15,000 year-end bonus.

What should Jane do?

### Solution

It is common for people to become ineligible for their bonuses when they leave a company. However, since the start date is fairly close to the end of the year, Jane should ask for a compensatory cash payment to make up for the bonus that she will leave behind.

### Sample Person-to-Person Script

JANE: Thank you for offering me the position at your company. I'm passionate about the role, and I'm excited to begin.

HIRING MANAGER: That's great to hear.

JANE: I would like to discuss the compensation with you before I accept. I'm satisfied with most of it, but if I leave my current job before December 15th, I will lose a $15,000 year-end bonus. I understand that you need me to join immediately. That's why I would like to request a signing bonus to make up for the loss.

HIRING MANAGER: I don't think we can give you a $15,000 signing bonus. It's too high.

JANE: Then could I get a $10,000 signing bonus? I would like to join the team, but I'm hesitant to leave that money on the table.

HIRING MANAGER: I'll see what I can do.

JANE: Thank you.

## Sample Email Script

Dear Hiring Manager,

Thank you for offering me the position at your company. I'm passionate about the role, and I'm excited to start working.

Before I accept however, I would like to discuss compensation with you. Because I am leaving before December 15th, I will become ineligible for my $15,000 year-end bonus. I want to join the company soon, but I am hesitant to leave that money on the table. I worked all year for that bonus. That is why I would like to ask for a $15,000 signing bonus to make up for that loss. Thanks for your consideration, and I look forward to hearing your response.

Sincerely,

Jane

## Case 21: What should I do if I need healthcare coverage before the company can offer it?

### Story

Getting health insurance is a high priority for Jane. Jane's family was covered by her husband's health insurance while he was working. However, when Jane's husband became injured and couldn't work, Jane needed to find a job with health insurance that would cover herself, her husband, and their two kids.

She's currently interviewing at a large company and believes that she'll receive an offer. However, she won't be eligible for their healthcare program until after she works six months on the job.

What should she do?

### Solution

Jane should ask for a signing bonus to buy private insurance for the six months that her family won't be covered. Most companies don't have the flexibility to diverge from a set corporate healthcare policy, but Jane can get a signing bonus and use that money to buy healthcare.

Prior to the negotiation, Jane should draw up an estimate of how much private healthcare would cost for six months for her family. Jane is more likely to convince the recruiter to give her a signing bonus if her argument is backed by evidence and research.

### Sample Person-to-Person Script

JANE: Thank you for offering me the position. I'm excited to begin working here. Before I can accept however, I would like to discuss the compensation.

RECRUITER: Of course. What would you like to talk about?

JANE: I think that the salary is fair and the other benefits are great, but I was disappointed with the healthcare program.

RECRUITER: Oh? We think that our healthcare benefits are competitive and typically outperforms our peer set.

JANE: Based on my research, I agree. However, I can't go without health insurance for my family for six months. I have a request: Can I be eligible as soon as I start working instead of waiting for half a year?

RECRUITER: I'm not sure that we can do that. Our corporate healthcare policy is pretty rigid. The delay in coverage is necessary to complete all of the paperwork and applications needed to get your family covered.

JANE: In that case, may I get a signing bonus to purchase short-term health insurance until my family is eligible for the health care coverage here?

RECRUITER: How much are you asking for?

JANE: My research indicates that it will cost about $600 a month for six months. So I would like to request a $3,600 signing bonus.

RECRUITER: That seems reasonable. I'll send the revised offer to my manager for approval.

JANE: Thank you. Once the offer is approved and in writing, I'll accept the position.

## Sample Email Script

Dear Recruiter,

Thank you for offering me the position at this company. I was very excited to get the offer.

However, I would like to discuss the compensation with you. My main concern is that the healthcare benefits do not kick in until after six months of employment. Unfortunately, my family currently does not have healthcare and I can't afford waiting that long to cover my family. I understand that corporate healthcare plans are quite inflexible, so I would like to request a signing bonus to purchase short-term private healthcare until I am covered by the company. My research indicates that it will cost about $600 a month for six months, so I would like to request a $3,600 signing bonus.

Finding healthcare is one of my top priorities, so I hope we can come to a mutual agreement.

Thank you,

Jane

## Case 22: What should I do if I want to negotiate a bigger bonus?

### Story

Jane loves sales. She feels the adrenaline whenever she pushes a prospective client over the fence and gets them to buy her product. Her passion landed her a great sales position at a new company. She tried to negotiate salary but was told that each sales person has the same salary to maintain compensation equity. However, Jane believes that she is more qualified than the average sales person.

What should Jane do?

### Solution

Jane should ask for a larger annual bonus if she truly thinks that she is more qualified than her peers. She should be specific in what sets her apart from other candidates. She could also try asking the hiring manager what a candidate would need to be rewarded with a larger bonus than what she was offered. If she has the skills or performance needed to get the bigger bonus, she can explicitly tell her hiring manager. If she doesn't, then Jane knows how to achieve the compensation increase in the future.

### Sample Person-to-Person Script

JANE: Thank you for offering me the sales position. I'm excited to join the company.

HIRING MANAGER: You're welcome. We're glad you will join us. You are accepting, yes?

JANE: Well, before I accept, I want to conclude our compensation discussion. I understand that you want to maintain compensation equity by giving each sales person the same salary. However, there must be cases where you think a candidate is more qualified than the others and therefore earn a larger bonus. What kinds of skills would merit that kind of compensation increase?

HIRING MANAGER: Well, we would need proof that the candidate can succeed. They would need to be a top performer in their previous company. They need to demonstrate a desire and passion for doing outbound leads, which is something most sales representatives hate to do.

JANE: I believe that I can show you that I am worth the larger bonus. At my previous company, I won two awards for exceeding sales quotas. I also completed the Solution Selling training course last May. This shows that I'm a performer and committed to improving my sales skills.

HIRING MANAGER: You do have a point. I don't think anyone else has those kinds of experiences. It is quite impressive.

JANE: Thank you. I also handled outbound leads in my previous position. That wasn't a requirement for this position, so I didn't mention it previously. In addition, I excel at cold calling, managing booths, creating sales letters, and maintaining email contacts with my clients.

HIRING MANAGER: Well, I guess we should have asked about outbound leads as well. You really seem to be more qualified than others.

JANE: Thank you. Anyway, that is why I would like to request a 10% larger annual bonus than stated in my offer. I'm confident that I am worth the extra money.

HIRING MANAGER: I'll have to discuss this with my supervisors, and I will let you know what they say. Will you accept if this can be arranged?

JANE: Absolutely. Thank you.

## Sample Email Script

Dear Hiring Manager,

Thank you again for offering me the sales position at your company. I'm still excited to join and help the company reach its goals.

Before I accept however, I would like to conclude the salary discussion. I understand that you want to maintain compensation equity by giving each sales person the same salary, but I believe that I am more qualified than my peers. At my previous company, I won two awards for exceeding sales quotas. I also completed the Solution Selling training course last May. In addition, I excel at cold calling, managing booths, creating sales letters, and maintaining email contacts with my clients.

That is why I would like to request a 10% larger annual bonus than stated in my offer. If the above awards and certification are not enough to merit a larger bonus, I hope that we can discuss ways that I can reach the 10% goal. I'm confident that I am worth the extra money.

If this can be arranged, I will definitely accept this offer. I hope that we can come to a mutual agreement.

Thank you,

Jane

# Negotiating stock grants and options

## Case 23: I received an offer with stock options. What does that mean?

### Story

Jane is transitioning from college student to full time employee at a relatively new startup. She's overwhelmed with all of the new changes and processes she has to learn. It became worse when Jane looked over the compensation package. She saw that she was receiving equity in her new company. New to the business world, she's unsure what that means.

What should she do?

### Solution

Research equity compensation before commencing salary negotiations. This way, she can at least have a general understanding of employee equity so that she knows what the company is offering. However, employee equity is a complicated topic; the details vary by company. Jane should not hesitate to ask the recruiter questions, even if her questions make her feel naïve or uneducated. The company will understand and respect her for taking initiative to ask and learn what she doesn't know.

### Sample Person-to-Person Script

JANE: Thank you for offering me the position at your company. I'm excited about the role.

RECRUITER: Great! We're excited too.

JANE: May I ask you a few questions about the compensation?

RECRUITER: Of course.

JANE: I'm somewhat confused about the stock option package. I have done some preliminary research before this discussion, but I'm not sure what the details of the package mean. Could we take some time to discuss?

RECRUITER: Sure. I'll start with some basics to make sure we're on the same page.

## Sample Email Script

Dear Recruiter,

Thank you for the job offer. I'm very excited about the role.

I would like to ask you some questions about the compensation package. I'm somewhat confused about the equity component of my compensation. I conducted some research online to figure out what it means, but I still don't feel that I know enough.

Could we please set up a time to discuss? I'd like to solidify my understanding.

Thank you,

Jane

## Case 24: I have an offer with stock options. What questions should I ask?

### Story

Like most startups, Pinterest gave Jane a job offer with stock options. She's looking for more information about the stock option package.

What questions should Jane ask?

### Solution

The value of an employee equity plan can vary, based on the details. Use the information checklist below as a questions guide and clarify your employee equity plan.

# Employee Equity Checklist

The first two columns indicate the checklist item and description. Use the last column to track the value offered in your compensation package.

| Item | Description | Value |
|------|-------------|-------|
| **Stock grants** | This gives an employee a certain number of shares, as part of one's overall compensation. Stock grants usually have conditions attached, such as a vesting schedule or individual performance requirements. Stock grants are normally contrasted with stock options. | |
| **Stock equity** | This is a right to purchase stock at a particular price, usually below current market value. With stock options, employers give employees a chance to own a portion of the company and get rewarded when the company increases in value. Stock options are normally contrasted with stock grants. | |
| **Number of shares** | While it may seem like more is better, the value of each share is a critical number to know. Getting one share worth $1,000 is better than getting 100 shares worth ten cents each. | |
| **Percentage of the company the stock represents** | Stock usually comes with voting rights. The more stock you hold, the more voting power you'll have. With that voting power, a shareholder can influence major company decisions including corporate governance and the election of corporate directors. | |
| **Current shares** | This is the total shares issued to date. This is usually a misleading indicator of total shares in the company, primarily because the company has likely issued stock options to purchase shares to other individuals and organizations. As the stock options get exercised, the stock pool gets inflated, reducing the percentage ownership of existing shareholders. Instead, the more relevant number is fully diluted shares; it factors in future exercise of currently unissued shares. | |
| **Current value of shares** | This is the market value of the shares offered. In a public company, these numbers are determined by the market. For private companies, current value is estimated, based on the per share valuation during the last round of funding. | |

|  |  |
|---|---|
| **Exercise price of shares** | The exercise price at which you can purchase stock from the company. In general, the exercise price is going to be the current market price at the time you received the option. It is favorable when the current value of your shares increases above the exercise price. The exercise price is also known as the strike price. |
| **Fully diluted shares** | This includes the number of shares issued to founders ("Founder Stock"), the number of shares reserved for employees ("Employee Pool"), the number of shares issued or promised to other investors ("Convertible Notes"), and any warrants outstanding. Fully diluted shares is contrasted with current shares issued, which does not include future commitments to issue stock, such as warrants and shares reserved for the employee pool. |
| **Future value of shares** | This refers to the future value of the company. If the company is expected to grow, the value of the shares should also grow. |
| **Incentive stock options (ISO)** | Stock options that are only granted to employees. ISO's have favorable tax treatment, usually if shares acquired upon exercise are held for more than one year after exercise and two years after the ISO's grant date. This is contrasted with non-qualified stock options. |
| **Liquidation preference** | It states which investors get paid first and how much during a liquidation event. Preferred stock holders may get liquidation preference. |
| **Non-qualified stock options (NSO)** | These options can be granted to anyone including employees and directors. Contrasted with incentive stock options, NSOs do not have favorable tax treatment. |
| **Preferred stock** | Preferred stock is different from common stock in two ways. First, preferred stockholders have preference over monetary distributions, such as dividends or other distributions such as during an acquisition. Second, preferred stockholders may also be entitled to special dividends that may not be given to common stockholders. Typically, common stock is what employees typically receive when exercising stock options. |
| **Vesting schedule** | The vesting schedule refers to the amount of time you must work at a company before you get to exercise your stock options. A four year vesting schedule means you'll get 100 percent of your stock options after four years of employment. A typical vesting schedule is a four year vesting schedule with a one year cliff. A one year cliff means that you won't get any shares until the first anniversary of stock issuance. Employers use vesting schedules to encourage employees to stay at a company. |

# Sample Person-to-Person Script

JANE: I have a couple of questions about the equity compensation package. Do you mind if I ask?

RECRUITER: Of course. Ask away.

JANE: What percentage of the company would my 15,000 shares represent?

RECRUITER: In fully diluted terms, they would be 0.05 percent of the company.

JANE: My understanding is that these are stock options. Is that correct?

RECRUITER: Yes.

JANE: Could you please explain the vesting schedule?

RECRUITER: Of course. We have a standard vesting schedule of four years with a one year cliff. That means that after a year, 25 percent of your shares vest. Then for the next three years, your shares vest on a monthly basis. After four years, your shares will be 100 percent vested.

JANE: Are there any special vesting conditions?

RECRUITER: Can you give me an example of what you mean?

JANE: There are three vesting scenarios that I'm aware of: first, some companies have the right to buy back vested shares at the exercise price if you leave a company before a liquidity event. Second, some companies offer accelerated vesting when the company gets acquired. Third, some companies, after an acquisition, offer six months of additional vesting after acquisition.

RECRUITER: Yes, our company has a clause that says if you are terminated due to an IPO or a change in control, 100 percent of your options would be fully vested. You will have eighteen months to exercise your options.

JANE: Do you allow early exercise of options?

RECRUITER: Yes, you are eligible to exercise options before you have fully vested.

JANE: When can I sell my stock?

RECRUITER: Once you've vested, you can use our transferable stock option program to sell your options to designated financial institutions.

JANE: Why would I want to do that?

RECRUITER: By selling your stock options, you don't have to exercise your options to realize your stock option gains.

JANE: Ah, got it. How does your proposed equity plan compare to market averages?

RECRUITER: We benchmark our equity packages using websites like AngelList and Wealthfront. Marketing directors at similar companies range from .023% to .093%.

JANE: How was the exercise price determined?

RECRUITER: During our last round of financing, our common stock was valued at $2.15 per share.

JANE: I found that your company raised $200 million in your series F last May, bringing your total funding to $762.5 million. Is that correct?

RECRUITER: Yes.

JANE: how long will the current funding last?

RECRUITER: On average, we raise funding every 12-18 months, so I expect the next round to happen in that timeframe.

JANE: Do you have a policy of follow-on stock grants?

RECRUITER: We do have a follow-on stock policy. Follow-on stocks can be granted under one or more of the following situations: performance, promotion, and evergreen grants. If you make an exception contribution, then we feel that you deserve more equity. If you get promoted, we believe that you should get equity ownership that's in-line with market averages. Lastly, we believe in evergreen grants. Evergreen grants help us achieve employee retention objectives. They should be comparable to what you would get if you were to leave our company and join another firm.

JANE: That sounds great. Thank you for your time. May I evaluate the offer some more and get back to you by the end of the week?

RECRUITER: By the end of the week would be perfect.

## Sample Email Script

Dear Recruiter,

Thank you for offering me the position. I'm excited about the role, and I'm looking forward to joining a growing company.

Before I accept the offer, I have several questions about the equity portion of the package.

1. What percentage of the company would my shares represent, on a fully diluted basis?
2. Am I getting stock options or restricted stock?
3. What is the vesting schedule of my shares?
4. Are there special vesting conditions? That is, does vesting accelerate upon acquisition? Or will anything happen to my vested shares if I leave before the entire vesting schedule has been completed?
5. Do you allow early exercise of options?
6. When can I sell my stock?
7. Does my stock include preferred shares?
8. How does your proposed equity plan compare to market averages?
9. How was the exercise price determined? How does this compare to the price of preferred stock issued in the last round?
10. How much has the company raised?

11. How long will the current funding last?

12. Is there a policy on follow-on stock grants?

I plan to stay at this company for a long time, so I want to fully understand the stock plan.

Thanks for taking the time to answer my questions,

Jane

# Case 25: I received an offer with stock options. How should I value it, relative to other compensation such as base salary and signing bonus?

## Story

Apple offered Jane a HR Director position. Jane is disappointed by the low salary because it is about $10,000 less than her previous job, but the company claims that their stock option plan makes up for the less-than-competitive salary.

Apple's current share price is $115. Jane's incentive stock options give her the right to purchase 500 shares at $115. The stock options vest over two years around January of each year.

What should Jane do?

## Solution

Jane should analyze the value of the shares, using publicly available data.

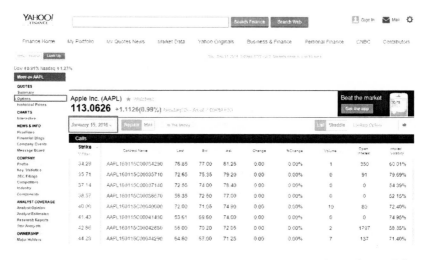

Screenshot / @Yahoo

Here's what we recommend:

1. Go to http://finance.yahoo.com/
2. Type Apple's stock ticker into the website's search box: AAPL
3. Select "Options" on the left hand navigation bar.
4. Choose the relevant dates.

In Jane's case, the relevant dates are:

| Date | Description | Price |
|------|-------------|-------|
| January 15, 2016 | Option price to buy one share at $115 | $12.80 |
| January 20, 2017 | Option price to buy one share at $115 | $19.30 |

Jane is given the right to purchase 500 shares total. We will assume half can be exercised on January 15, 2016; the other half can be exercised on January 20, 2017. Using the information above, we get the following:

| | | |
|------|-------------|-------|
| Value of 2016 stock options | $12.80 * 250 | $3,200 |
| Value of 2017 stock options | $19.30 * 250 | $4,825 |
| **Total Value** | | **$8,025** |

For candidates who are valuing stock options that do not have market data, use the Black-Scholes option pricing formula. This is beyond the scope of the book, so refer to a finance textbook or Wikipedia for more details.

## Sample Person-to-Person Script

JANE: Thank you for offering me the HR Director position at your company.

HIRING MANAGER: You're welcome.

JANE: You mentioned that my company equity makes up for the low salary. Could I ask you some questions about that?

HIRING MANAGER: Of course.

JANE: For the base salary, my research shows that your offer is $10,000 below the average. For the stock options, my calculations show that the stock option you gave me is worth around $8,000.

HIRING MANAGER: That's right.

JANE: The problem is that I don't want to take my chances on almost making a fair market salary. That is why I would like to request an additional $2,000 in my base salary. Then the $10,000 estimate, in addition to the $2,000, will ensure that I'm paid my fair value.

HIRING MANAGER: I see. I will have to discuss that with my boss.

JANE: Of course. When can I expect an answer from you?

HIRING MANAGER: In a couple of days. I'll let you know what my boss says.

JANE: Thank you. I appreciate it.

## Sample Person-to-Person Script

Dear Hiring Manager,

Thank you for offering me the HR Director position at Apple. I'm excited to be a part of the company and do my part to help the company reach its goals.

You mentioned that my company equity makes up for my low salary, but I have a few questions about this.

My research indicates that my stock options will worth around $8,000. I don't want to take my chances on almost making a fair market salary. That is why I would like to request an additional $2,000 in my base salary. Then the $8,000 stock options estimate, in addition to the $2,000, will ensure that I'm paid my fair value.

I'm confident that I can add a lot of value to your organization, so I hope you will consider my request.

Thank you,

Jane

## Case 26: What should I do if I am evaluating different stock options in different companies?

### Story

Jane is choosing between two companies, and she is largely indifferent to which company she chooses.

Company A is a small startup, and she has the option to purchase 15,000 shares at a strike price of $0.25 per share. The estimated value of her stock option package is $1.70 per share. Her base salary will be $150,000.

Company B is a public company, and she'll receive 5,000 restricted stock units valued at $10 per share. Her base salary will be $175,000.

Both companies have a four year vesting policy, with a straight 25 percent vesting each year. Both options represent 0.2 percent of the company's shares.

However, Jane is more confident in Company A's ability to succeed and grow.

Which one should Jane choose?

### Solution

| Offer | Salary | Equity | | Equity Value | Total Value |
|-------|--------|--------|--|--------------|-------------|
| A | $150,000 | Option: | 15,000 shares * $1.70 | $25,500 | $175,500 |
| B | $175,000 | Grant: | 5,000 shares * $10 | $50,000 | $225,000 |

Based on total value, offer B appears to be more attractive. However, that doesn't factor in potential equity upside. If Jane believes that company A has more equity upside, then B's offer may not be as attractive.

### Sample Person-to-Person Script

JANE: Thank you for offering me the position at Company A.

HIRING MANAGER: You're welcome. Are you ready to accept the offer?

JANE: Not quite. I prefer to work for Company A, but Company B has offered me a very attractive offer. Company B's compensation is worth around $225,000 including the base salary and stock options, but your offer is only work around $175,500. I understand that Company A is a startup and can't afford to pay as much as a large company, but I would like to discuss creative ways to bridge the gap between the two offers.

HIRING MANAGER: What did you have in mind?

JANE: I would like to request a vesting schedule of three years and an extra week of vacation days.

HIRING MANAGER: That's an interesting proposal. I'll have to discuss it with the founders. Could I give you an answer in a couple of days?

JANE: Of course. Thank you for considering my request.

## Sample Email Script

Dear Hiring Manager,

Thank you for offering me the position at Company A. I'm excited to work for an early-stage startup and see how I can impact the company.

Before I accept, I would like to discuss the compensation package. I currently have another offer from Company B. Their compensation package is around $225,000 including the base salary and stock option plan. I found that in total, Company A's compensation package is valued at around $175,500. I understand that Company A is a startup and can't afford to pay as much as a large company, but I would like to discuss creative ways to bridge the gap between the two offers.

I would like to request a vesting schedule of three years and an extra week of vacation days. I'm confident that I can bring a lot of value to Company A, so I hope that we can come to a mutual agreement.

Thank you,

Jane

## Case 27: I received an offer with stock options. How can I find out if it is a competitive plan?

### Story

Jane received an offer for a product manager position at a Silicon Valley startup. The salary and benefits are reasonable, but Jane wants to know how her stock option package compares to other startups. They tell her that it is a very competitive stock option package, but she wants to verify it herself. Since Jane doesn't have any competing offers, she needs an alternate method to assess her offer.

What should Jane do?

### Solution

Jane can utilize a resource called AngelList (https://angel.co/salaries) to compare her stock options to options granted by other start-ups'. AngelList compiles equity data for different positions and makes it easy to search based on location, skill, role, or market. Jane can search based on her characteristics and find comparable stock option data that she can use in her negotiations.

### Sample Person-to-Person Script

JANE: May I ask you some additional questions about the stock option package?

HIRING MANAGER: Of course. What else do you want to know?

JANE: What percentage of the company will my shares represent?

HIRING MANAGER: About 0.08 percent of the company.

JANE: That seems low compared to other startups in the area.

HIRING MANAGER: What do you mean?

JANE: According to my research, the average product manager receives at least 0.1 percent of the company. Since I have more years of experience than the average product manager, I would like to request the equivalent number of shares so that my ownership of the company is 0.14 percent. It is on the mid-to-high end of the stock values offered in Silicon Valley for product managers.

HIRING MANAGER: That is quite a jump from the original 0.08 percent.

JANE: Yes, it is. But I know that I can bring that extra value and expertise that will benefit the company in the future.

HIRING MANAGER: Okay. I'll send the request for an increase in your stock option package. We'll see what happens.

## Sample Email Script

Dear Hiring Manager,

Thank you again for offering me the Product Manager position. Before I accept, I would like to discuss the stock option plan with you. You mentioned that my percentage of the shares is 0.08 percent, but according to my research, the average product manager usually receives at least 0.1 percent of the company. Since I have more years of experience than the average product manager, I would like to request the appropriate shares to make my ownership percentage 0.14 percent. It is on the mid-to-high end of stock values offered to Silicon Valley product managers.

I'm really excited about this role, and I hope that we can come to a mutual agreement. I'm confident that I can bring extra value and expertise that will benefit the company in the future.

Thank you,

Jane

# Negotiating an early review

## Case 28: What should I do if I want an early review?

### Story

Jane is in negotiations with a prospective company about her compensation package. She thinks she's worth more money, so she asks for a six percent higher salary. Unfortunately, the company won't budge. They say that she's got great people skills and performed well on the interview, but she's an otherwise unknown quantity when it comes to on the job performance.

What should Jane do?

### Solution

Jane should ask the company if she can get an early review. This way, she can earn the extra money. If she doesn't meet the performance criteria established for the early review, then the company doesn't have to pay extra money. It is a win-win situation for her and the company.

### Sample Person-to-Person Script

JANE: Thank you again for offering me the position. I would like to revisit the question of compensation.

HIRING MANAGER: Sorry, we can't give you the six percent raise.

JANE: Can I propose an alternative solution?

HIRING MANAGER: Sure.

JANE: I would like to request an early performance review in six months. At that time, if my performance merits it, I would like a salary adjustment.

HIRING MANAGER: That's an interesting proposal.

JANE: This will be a win-win situation for both of us. I'll work to provide more value to the company. If I don't meet the criteria we establish together, then you won't have to pay me more.

HIRING MANAGER: I like that idea. It will give you a chance to show us your capabilities. Let me discuss this with my supervisor and then we can talk about the goals for your early review.

JANE: That sounds great. Thank you.

## Sample Email Script

Dear Hiring Manager,

Thank you for offering me the position at your company. I'm very interested in the position, and I'm passionate about the company.

Before I accept however, I would like to discuss compensation again. I understand that you're hesitant to give me the six percent salary increase because I haven't proven my performance on the job. That is why I would like to request an early review six months from my start date. I'm confident that I can prove to you that I am worth the six percent increase in salary.

I hope we can come to a mutual agreement. I'm excited to begin working at your company.

Thank you,

Jane

# Case 29: What should I do if I can't make the start date at a new job?

## Story

Jane is currently working at a company on the East Coast. She recently received a job offer in California for a position that she is really passionate about. However, the company wants her to start her first day next week. Jane cannot make that deadline for a variety of reasons. First, she has to give her current company at least two weeks' notice before she can quit. Second, she needs a week to take care of personal errands including selling her car, finding a new place to live, and terminating her current lease.

Jane wants to accept the new offer, but she can't possibly start in a week.

What should Jane do?

## Solution

Jane should ask her new company to move her start date back two weeks so that she has time to prepare for the big move. Jane should be prepared to explain her situation. If the new company can't push the date back, Jane should also try to negotiate with both companies. Perhaps she can work part-time for the last two weeks. Jane can spend half the day tending to her duties at work, and she can spend the remainder getting ready for the big move. Or Jane could work from the East Coast for a couple of weeks before she fully relocates.

## Sample Person-to-Person Script

JANE: Thank you for offering me the position at the San Francisco branch. I'm excited about the role.

HIRING MANAGER: You're welcome. I'm excited for you to join.

JANE: Unfortunately, I can't make the requested start date.

HIRING MANAGER: Oh? I thought a week would be enough time. We really need you here.

JANE: I need to give my current boss two weeks' notice before I leave. I also need to sell my car and find a new place to live in San Francisco.

HIRING MANAGER: There are meetings I wanted you to be a part of in two weeks. Is there any way you can come?

JANE: Based on my previous relocation experiences, I don't feel comfortable with this timetable. When I join the company, I want to give it my full attention and focus, and I can't do that if I have personal loose ends. As a compromise, maybe I can join the team meetings via Skype or conference call?

HIRING MANAGER: I guess we could do that. How long are you exactly asking for?

JANE: I would like to start in three weeks, two weeks after the requested date.

HIRING MANAGER: Alright. I'll push things back. I'll also let you know when to be available for the conference calls. Anything else?

JANE: No, that is all. Thank you.

## Sample Email Script

Dear Hiring Manager,

Thank you for offering me the position at the San Francisco branch. Unfortunately, I can't make the requested start date. I actually need to give my current boss two weeks' notice before I leave. I also need at least a week to straighten out my life here and find a new place to live in San Francisco. That is why I would like to start in three weeks, two weeks after the requested start date.

I really want to join your company, but I can't possibly come before then. I hope that we can come to a mutual agreement.

Thank you,

Jane

# Negotiating more vacation time

## Case 30: What should I do if I want to negotiate for more vacation time?

### Story

Jane received an offer from a 300-person online retailer. She's pleased with the base salary; it's a $30,000 increase from her base salary of $150,000.

However, the compensation package only includes two weeks of vacation. She's accustomed to a three week vacation. She takes a week off to spend time with parents and in-laws during Thanksgiving and Christmas respectively. She also takes a week off for summer vacation.

What should she do?

### Solution

Jane can offer to brainstorm without risk with the negotiating party. By brainstorming possible solutions with her recruiter, they can discuss options without commitment and find a solution that works for both of them. It does not matter that Jane does not know why the vacation is set to two weeks by default or whether or not she can convince the recruiter to give her more.

### Sample Person-to-Person Script

HIRING MANAGER: Sorry, I can't give you three weeks of vacation.

JANE: Why not?

HIRING MANAGER: Two weeks is the standard vacation for candidates at your level.

JANE: Does the standard vacation rate change over time?

HIRING MANAGER: Yes, after three years in your role, your standard vacation would increase from two weeks to three.

JANE: What would be wrong with providing three weeks of vacation now?

HIRING MANAGER: I have to carefully consider equality in the organization and how it might affect morale. I also need to be careful and not set a precedent. I also need to be mindful about whether I am unwittingly setting a precedent.

JANE: So you're concerned about compensation equity.

HIRING MANAGER: Yes.

JANE: Are you concerned about anything else?

HIRING MANAGER: No.

JANE: Do you mind if we brainstorm some potential solutions?

HIRING MANAGER: What's the point?

JANE: I want to see if there are creative ways we can reach agreement.

HIRING MANAGER: I'm not ready to commit to anything.

JANE; There's no commitment necessary. I just want to brainstorm with you for five minutes to see if we can come up with something creative. You'll have veto power over whatever proposals we discuss.

I'll start first. Since I am coming from a company similar to yours, we could count my years at my current employer toward tenure at your company. We'll call that option A. Your turn.

HIRING MANAGER: You could have the third week off, but with no pay.

JANE: We'll call that option B. I'll go next. You could adjust the policy so that everyone at my level gets three weeks of vacation after one year, not three. We'll call this option C.

HIRING MANAGER: I see.

JANE: From your point of view, what are the pros and cons of each option?

HIRING MANAGER: For option A, it'll meet your needs, but others on the team will be unhappy about not getting credit for their time at previous employers. The fair thing to do is extending credit to them too. That would trigger extra vacation for dozens of employees at the company, increasing my costs.

JANE: I see. How about option B?

HIRING MANAGER: Option B is promising because it meets your needs without increasing my costs. Other folks on the team are also likely to see that option as being fair. Option C feels similar to Option A. The difference I see is that you would have one less week of vacation this year. It would also increase my costs, but only for current and future employees who have not reached the three year tenure mark.

JANE: Are you comfortable with giving me option B?

HIRING MANAGER: Sure, we can include that in your employment contract.

## Sample Email Script

Dear Hiring Manager,

Thank you again for offering me the position. I'm very excited about the role.

However, I would like to return to compensation. I make it one of my priorities to spend time with my family, so I would like to reexamine my request for another week of vacation. You said that two weeks is standard. I have a suggestion. I would like to brainstorm some ways that we can bridge the gap between your policy and my request. I'm sure that there is a creative agreement we can reach.

Option A: Since I am coming from a company that is similar to yours, we could count my years at my current employer toward tenure at yours. Then I can receive three weeks a little earlier than normal.

Option B: I could have the third week off without pay.

Option C: You could adjust the policy so that everyone at my level gets three weeks of vacation after one year, not three.

If you have other options, I would love to hear them. I hope my suggestions have been useful when thinking about how I can receive an extra week of vacation without violating your policy. I look forward to hearing your response.

Thank you,

Jane

# Negotiating flexible hours

## Case 31: What should I do if I want to negotiate flexible hours?

### Story

Jane was recently offered a great position at a prestigious company. The hours are a typical office job of 9 a.m. to 5 p.m. At her current job, she works 7 a.m. to 3 p.m. to go and pick up her kids from daycare at 3:30 p.m. She makes it a priority to spend time with her kids, especially since they haven't entered school yet.

What should Jane do?

### Solution

Jane should ask her prospective employer for a work schedule that complements her kids' schedule. Flexible working hours is a perk that won't cost the company extra money.

### Sample Person-to-Person Script

JANE: Thank you again for offering me the position.

HIRING MANAGER: You're welcome. So will you be joining us?

JANE: I would like to, but I want to talk about some aspects of the job first.

HIRING MANAGER: Sure.

JANE: I was wondering if there was any flexibility in the job hours.

HIRING MANAGER: Well, most people work the regular hours in the office, but there's no policy against it. What did you have in mind?

JANE: I would like to work 7 a.m. to 3 p.m. so that I can pick up my kids from daycare. It is still the full eight hours, but I would just come and leave earlier.

HIRING MANAGER: I guess a two hour difference wouldn't impact the other team members very much. You would have to remind everyone so that meetings are scheduled earlier in the day.

JANE: I can definitely do that.

HIRING MANAGER: Why don't we do a test run for a couple of months and make sure that it works. If everything still runs smoothly, I'll let you work the hours you want. Otherwise, you will work the same hours as everyone else.

JANE: Thanks for agreeing to the pilot run.

## Sample Email Script

Dear Hiring Manager,

Thank you for offering me the position. I'm excited about the role, and I hope that I can start soon.

However, I would like to discuss the working hours with you. At my current job, I work 7 a.m. to 3 p.m. It allows me to pick up my kids from daycare. It is still an eight hour workday, but I come two hours earlier and leave two hours earlier. I would like to continue this work schedule with this new role. I think that the work place allows flexibility. My meetings would just have to be scheduled earlier. I was able to make it work in my current job and I'm confident that I can make it work in the new one as well. I can also be flexible when it comes to meetings and conference calls away from the office, so that my flexible work schedule doesn't unnecessarily affect others' productivity.

I hope we can come to an agreement. I value the time I have with my kids before they become school-aged. I hope you understand my request.

Thank you,

Jane

## Case 32: What should I do if I want to work from home a couple days a week?

### Story

Jane was recently offered a position as a lead software developer at a new company. She currently lives only ten minutes away from her office, but now will have to drive fifty minutes to get to her new office. She is really passionate about her new position and wants to accept it, but she's wary of the longer commute. As a software developer, Jane knows that some companies allow their employees to work remotely.

What should Jane do?

### Solution

Jane should ask her prospective employer if she can work from home at least once a week. This way she can save on gas and time by telecommuting. Letting Jane work from home will satisfy Jane without costing the company any money.

### Sample Person-to-Person Script

JANE: Thank you for offering me the software developer position at your company.

HIRING MANAGER: You're welcome. Are you ready to accept the offer?

JANE: Not quite. May I ask you a few questions about the work environment?

HIRING MANAGER: Of course.

JANE: Would you say that someone in my position could do their work remotely? At home for example?

HIRING MANAGER: I would say so. There are some days where we have meetings, so you couldn't work from home. But on other days, I don't see why you couldn't work from home.

148

JANE: I see. Then I would like to request working from home one day a week. My commute will increase from ten to fifty minutes if I take this job. A longer commute means spending more time away from work and family as well as more money for gas.

HIRING MANAGER: Which day do you want to work from home?

JANE: I'm flexible about the day of the week I would work from home. I just want a day that is most convenient for everyone.

HIRING MANAGER: That sounds fair. Sure, you can work from home one day a week, with the exact day of the week to be decided.

JANE: Great! Thank you.

## Sample Email Script

Dear Hiring Manager,

Thank you for offering me the software developer position. I'm excited about the role, and I'm confident that I can bring a lot of value to the company.

Before I can accept the offer, I would like to discuss compensation with you. I think that the salary is fair and in-line with the market value of this position, but I would like to discuss some possible changes in the benefits. While I am happy with the base salary, I am hesitant to accept the offer because of the increased commute to the office from my home. Taking this new job will increase my daily drive from ten to fifty minutes. To save time, I would like to request a day every week to work from home instead of at the office. I can perform my job adequately at home while saving time and gas on my commute. This arrangement will not cost the company more money. Of course, we can discuss which day would be most convenient for everybody. I'm confident that we can come to a mutual agreement.

Thank you,

Jane

# Negotiating other things

## Case 33: What should I do if I want to ask the company to pay for my tuition?

### Story

Jane tried to negotiate salary with her recruiter, but she hasn't had any success. It doesn't matter if it is base salary or signing bonus; they're telling her that it's about "compensation equity." They say that they can't give her more benefits and money than her peers.

There's one more thing she'd like to try: tuition reimbursement. Getting her MBA has always been a dream of hers, and she's curious if they're willing to pay for it. It would definitely seal the deal for her.

What should Jane say?

### Solution

Jane should ask for tuition reimbursement. She should acknowledge the state of their negotiations first so that the recruiter knows that she's not intentionally being difficult. Then she can offer the tuition reimbursement as a way to bridge the gap between their offer and her market value. She will most likely have to agree to a payback clause if her company does pay for her tuition. The company doesn't want to pay for an employee's tuition just to have them quit and work somewhere else.

If she frames her new degree as added value for the company, she's more likely to succeed. Her increased education would make her a more valuable employee.

### Sample Person-to-Person Script

JANE: I understand that the salary and bonuses are non-negotiable, so, I would like to request a tuition reimbursement to go back to school and get an MBA.

RECRUITER: Where did you have in mind?

JANE: I want to get my MBA from Northwestern University's Kellogg School of Management's Executive MBA Program. I've researched the costs and it will cost a total of $173,610 spread out over two years. I realize that's a lot of money, so I would like to get reimbursed for half. That's $43,400 per year. By getting my MBA, I'll be a more valuable employee because I can apply my new knowledge to my job.

RECRUITER: That's an interesting proposal. I'll see if I can get this approved by my supervisor.

*The recruiter calls Jane the next day.*

RECRUITER: Hi Jane. I talked to my supervisors about the tuition reimbursement, and they have agreed to pay for half of the tuition. However, you will have to pay the company back if you leave the company within two years of getting your MBA.

JANE: Great! That sounds fair. I don't plan on leaving the company any time soon. Thank you.

## Sample Email Script

Dear Recruiter,

Thank you again for offering me the position at this company. I would like to emphasize that I'm still interested in the role, but I would like to discuss compensation a little more.

I understand that the salary and bonuses are non-negotiable, so I would like to request a tuition reimbursement to go back to school and get an MBA from the Northwestern University's Kellogg School of Management. I've researched the costs, and it will cost a total of $66,987 spread out over three years. Since $173,610 is a lot of money, I would like to get reimbursed for half of the tuition cost. That will be about $43,400 a year. By getting my MBA, I'll be a more valuable employee because I can apply new knowledge to my job.

I'm eager to accept the offer, and I hope that we can come to a mutually beneficial agreement.

Thank you,

Jane

# Case 34: What should I do if I need relocation assistance?

## Story

Jane is currently living in San Diego as an Operations Lead. She recently got a job offer to work in New York as a Director of Operations. She really wants to take the job, but the relocation expenses would be enormous. First, her current lease still has three months left; her landlord will take her $2,000 security deposit if she breaks her lease. Second, she needs to find a place to live in New York, and it is infamous for its exorbitant rent. Third, she will pay to move her furniture and belongings across the country.

What should Jane do?

## Solution

Jane should ask for a relocation allowance to cover moving costs. The money may seem like a lot to her, but it may not be for the company, who might find it difficult to find a similar candidate, at any price.

## Sample Person-to-Person Script

JANE: Thank you for offering me the Director of Operations position in New York. I'm excited about the role, and the opportunity to advance my career.

HIRING MANAGER: Of course. We're excited to have you on board.

JANE: If you don't mind, I would like to discuss my compensation package with you.

HIRING MANAGER: Sure, was it not satisfactory?

JANE: I'm satisfied with most of the package. I thought that the base salary and benefits were fair and appropriate for the position and my qualifications. However, I would like a relocation allowance of $18,000.

HIRING MANAGER: I see. What will $18,000 cover?

JANE: This will cover the loss of my security deposit for my current home, the broker fees for finding a new apartment, the cost to move my belongings, and a plane ticket.

HIRING MANAGER: That seems fair. Let me ask HR if they can approve an $18,000 relocation package for you.

JANE: Thank you.

## Sample Email Script

Dear Hiring Manager,

Thank you for offering me the Director of Operations position in New York. I'm excited about the role and the opportunity to advance my career.

Before I accept however, I would like to discuss my compensation. I'm satisfied with most of the package. I thought that the base salary and benefits were fair and appropriate for the position and my qualifications. However, I would like to request an $18,000 relocation allowance. This will cover the loss of my security deposit for my current home, the broker fees for finding a new apartment, the cost to move my belongings, and a plane ticket.

I'm very excited about the position, and I'm confident that I am a good fit. I know that I can add a lot of value. The relocation assistance would ease the transition to a new job and a new city.

Thank you,

Jane

## Case 35: What should I do if the recruiter won't negotiate because the previous person didn't negotiate?

### Story

Jane has offer for a nine month contractor position as a business analyst at $100 per hour. Jane is looking for a salary of $120 per hour.

Jane attempts to negotiate with the recruiter, but she gets rebuffed. The recruiter replies that the previous analyst did not negotiate and simply accepted it. The recruiter goes on to explain that if that person accepted the same exact job, with similar qualifications, then why should the recruiter offer more for the same job?

What should Jane say?

### Solution

For candidates who aren't familiar with confrontation, they may perceive this push back as a rejection. However, candidates need to be prepared for objections and figure out how to reply successfully.

In this scenario, the candidate can respond with the following:

- **The job market has changed**. "What was true when the previous candidate held the job is no longer true now. The talent market has gotten hotter, and my skills are in demand. My research indicates that what I'm asking for is reasonable."
- **Different candidates, different needs.** "While it may be the same position, no two individuals are alike. I imagine the previous person had different experiences and qualifications than I do. We also have unique situations and different needs, so our compensation packages should be independent of each other."
- **Competing job offers.** "I have another offer for a similar position at $120 per hour. I would like to join your company,

but I cannot in good conscience do so when I know there's a 20% difference in pay."

- **Increased cost of living.** "I don't know when the last candidate negotiated his offer with your company. However, I do know that housing costs in the area have increased 10% since last year."

## Sample Person-to-Person Script

JANE: I don't think that it's fair to compare my situation with the previous employee.

RECRUITER: Why is that?

JANE: The last contractor was hired in 2007, about seven years ago. Since then, inflation has risen by 15 percent. If I was paid the same $100 as the last employee, I would have a lower standard of living due to increased prices.

RECRUITER: Then would $115 per hour satisfy you?

JANE: I would like to get closer to my $120 per hour goal.

RECRUITER: $120 is a bit higher than what we have budgeted for.

JANE: If you can do $118, I'll be ready to accept.

RECRUITER: Okay. I'll tentatively say that I can do $118 an hour, but I will have to get it approved by the hiring manager first. I'll get that in writing as soon as possible and send it to you.

JANE: Thank you. I really appreciate your time and I'm glad we could come to a mutual agreement. I'll wait to hear back from you.

## Sample Email Script

Dear Hiring Manager,

Thank you for offering me the contractor position at your company. I'm excited to begin contributing to your company's goals. Before I accept the offer, I would like to discuss compensation with you. Your recruiter stated that the last contractor did not negotiate, so the set wage is $100 an hour. However, I don't think that it's fair to compare my situation with the previous employee. The last contractor was hired in 2007, about seven years ago. Since then, inflation has raised prices by 15 percent. If I was paid the same $100 as the last employee, I would have a lower standard of living due to increased prices. Because I have a $120 goal, I would like to request an hourly wage increase of $18 above your offer, making my base wage $118.

I'm confident that I can add value to your organization, and I hope that we can come to an agreement.

Thank you,

Jane

## Case 36: What should I do if I want to ask the company to pay for my childcare costs?

### Story

Jane is a single mom working in the suburbs located east of her house. Her child's daycare center is situated right beside her office, so she can easily pick up her son on her way home. However, Jane was recently offered a new position at a prestigious company in the city west of her home.

She really wants to take the job, but she would also have to change to a closer daycare since her current one would be out of the way. The city day care will also be more expensive. Her current child care arrangement costs $5,500 per year, but an equivalent child care in the city will cost $7,000 per year. To reduce her out of pocket costs for taking the new job, Jane wants to ask for a childcare allowance.

How should she ask?

### Solution

Sensitive to the needs of working families, a child care allowance is a perk that a HR partner will consider. If you do your research and show how much extra money switching jobs will cost you, your recruiter will more likely grant you the allowance.

### Sample Person-to-Person Script

JANE: Thank you for your offer. I'm very interested in working for this company.

HR PARTNER: You're welcome. Are you happy with the compensation package?

JANE: Overall, I am happy. However, I realized that I would have to change child care centers. My current job allows me to utilize a quality day care center next to my office, but if I move, I will have to relocate my son to a more expensive center in the city. I would like a childcare allowance to pay for the increased costs of relocating my toddler.

HR PARTNER: I see. How much are you looking for?

JANE: Well I'm most interested in the Sunshine Preschool. It is on the way back home and is highly recommended. The total cost for the year will be $7,000.

HR PARTNER: $7,000 is a bit more than we have available in our budget. What is the price of your current child care arrangement?

JANE: It is around $5,500 a year.

HR PARTNER: Perhaps we can try a $1,500 allowance. It'll bridge the gap between the old and new child care center. How does that sound? Of course, I'll have to get this approved by the CEO first.

JANE: Let's give it a try. I look forward to hearing from you soon.

## Sample Email Script

Dear HR Partner,

Thank you for offering me the position at this company. I'm very excited about the role.

However, I would like to discuss compensation with you first. I realized that I would have to change child care centers. My current job allows me to utilize a quality day care center next to my office, but if I move, I will have to relocate my son to a more expensive center in the city. I would like a childcare allowance to pay for the increased costs of relocating my toddler.

For the current preschool, the annual child care cost is $5,500. I found a new child care center, where the annual cost is $7,000. Can you pay the incremental $1,500 annual costs I would incur if I took this job?

Finding a quality program for my son is one of my top priorities, so I hope we can come to an agreement.

Thank you,

Jane

## Case 37: What to do if I want a severance package before I get hired?

### Story

Jane received a job offer as chief financial officer (CFO) of a medium-sized company after being laid off the year before due to a merger. She suffered financially because her previous company didn't give out severance packages. Now she fears facing that again. However, when Jane looked over her compensation package, there was once again no mention of a severance package in case she was let go.

What should Jane do?

### Solution

Jane won't get what she wants if she doesn't ask for it. It is a delicate discussion. A request for a severance package signals an unsavory end, even before she begins. However, it is common for executives. Executive roles have high turnover. And the limited supply of executive roles makes it difficult to find a job immediately after termination.

Here's an example severance clause:

*Severance without Change of Control*

*If you are terminated without Cause or you resign your employment due to a Constructive Termination, so long as such termination is not within twelve (12) months following a Change of Control, then you shall be entitled to receive, as severance, (a) six (6) month's base salary continuation, (b) six (6) months reimbursement of payments for continuing health coverage, pursuant to COBRA, assuming you elect COBRA continuation, and (c) continued vesting of your shares for a period of three (3) months following such employment termination. Your right to such salary continuation, COBRA reimbursement, and continued vesting is conditioned upon your signing the Company's then current standard form of release releasing the Company (or any successor entity), its officers, directors and affiliates from all liability whatsoever.*

161

*For clarity purposes, you shall not be entitled to any bonus after any such termination, nor shall you be entitled to any acceleration of vesting of your stock options.*

Source: SEC Filings, Offer Letter for Jeffrey Weiner, CEO of LinkedIn

Despite the potential awkwardness, having a severance clause in your offer letter is important, especially for senior executives.

## Sample Person-to-Person Script

JANE: Thank you for offering me the CFO position. I'm excited about the job, and I'm confident that I can bring a lot of value to the company.

HIRING MANAGER: You're welcome.

JANE: Before I can accept, I would like to discuss the lack of a severance package. Do you normally give out severance packages?

HIRING MANAGER: We usually do. But it seems a bit odd that you would ask for this before you start. Our company determines the severance package when the situation arises.

JANE: Well, I'm very thorough, so I would like to solidify severance package terms in advance.

HIRING MANAGER: I see.

JANE: I am requesting that six months' worth of wages and health and dental insurance coverage for twelve months is a typical and appropriate severance package.

HIRING MANAGER: That seems aggressive. I was thinking closer to three months.

JANE: I researched how long it takes CFOs at medium sized companies to find a new role. It ranges from six to twelve months. This data point is in-line with my own experience. I looked for twelve months before landing this current role.

HIRING MANGER: You raise a good point. I'll discuss this with HR, and I'll keep you apprised of next steps.

## Sample Email Script

Dear Hiring Manager,

Thank you for offering me the position. I'm excited about the job, and I'm confident that I can bring a lot of value to the company.

Before I can accept, I would like to discuss the lack of a severance package. I'm very thorough, so I would like to solidify the severance package terms in advance. I believe that six months' worth of wages and health and dental insurance coverage for nine months is a typical and appropriate severance package.

This is my only request regarding the compensation package. I would be happy to discuss this further.

I'm very excited about the role, and I can't wait to begin.

Thank you,

Jane

## Case 38: What should I do if I want to negotiate for H-1B sponsorship?

### Story

Jane is a MBA student from Turkey who is completing business school in the United States. She is currently staying in the United States on a student visa, but unfortunately it is going to expire soon since she is going to graduate in a few months. Since Jane studies business strategy, she is interested in Bellevue Consulting Group's strategy manager role. Jane wants to work in the United States, but would need an H-1B visa to stay in the country.

What should she do?

### Solution

Jane should interview for the position and see if the company would be willing to sponsor an H-1B visa for her. An H-1B visa allows a foreign national to work at the company. Employees can only be eligible if they have a bachelor's degree or higher degree of education and if their job requires the use of that degree. Companies ordinarily sponsor candidates for H-1B visas if there are no viable domestic candidates. This is because the H-1B sponsorship requires expensive application and lawyer fees.

### Sample Person-to-Person Script

*The recruiter calls Jane a few days after she expresses interest.*

RECRUITER: Hello, Jane. I understand that you are interested in Bellevue's strategy manager role.

JANE: Yes, that is correct.

RECRUITER: Great! I reviewed your resume, and I think you might be a great fit with our organization. Could I ask you some preliminary questions before we set up an interview time?

JANE: Of course.

RECRUITER: In your application, you indicated that you are authorized to work now. However, you would require sponsorship to continue working in the United States. Is that correct?

JANE: Yes, that's right. I'm currently in business school, so I'm in the United States with a student visa. Since I'm graduating in a few months, my visa will soon expire. That's why I need sponsorship in my next job to continue working in this country. More specifically, I would like H-1B sponsorship because I have an advanced education, and I would like to utilize my education in my career.

RECRUITER: You are probably aware that the H-1B visa is only available for six years total. What do you plan on doing once you get reach that six year maximum?

JANE: I am probably going to apply for a green card to become a permanent resident.

RECRUITER: That seems like a good plan. While we currently don't have H-1B sponsorship readily available for our employees, we've had some trouble finding qualified candidates. Perhaps you would be a good fit for our company. Would you still be interested in coming in for an interview even if we can't guarantee sponsorship?

JANE: Of course! I'm sure that we can come to an agreement if we find that I'm the best candidate for the position.

RECRUITER: Excellent! Let me pull up my calendar.

*A few days after her successful interview, Jane meets the hiring manager again.*

HIRING MANAGER: It was great meeting you, Jane, but unfortunately we cannot extend the position to you. We thought you were highly qualified and good fit for Bellevue Consulting Group, but we just don't have the money to sponsor your H-1B visa at this time.

JANE: Was that the only reason that I didn't get the job?

HIRING MANAGER: Yes, it was.

JANE: Then could we discuss ways that we can create a situation that works for both of us?

HIRING MANAGER: Sure. Do you have any ideas?

JANE: I could cover some of the costs of getting the visa. I'm passionate about the company and the industry, so I'm willing to spend my own money to stay here and work.

HIRING MANAGER: That's an interesting proposal. You do seem very determined to join Bellevue Consulting Group.

JANE: How much would I need to pay out of pocket?

HIRING MANAGER: The total cost would be $5,550, but the company is willing to pay $3,500. That still leaves $2,050.

JANE: That is a little more money than I can pay upfront right now. Could the $2,050 be garnished from my wages?

HIRING MANAGER: That seems like an appropriate solution. We would love to have you join us. I'll discuss it with my superiors, and I'll let you know what they say.

JANE: Sounds perfect. I look forward to hearing back from you.

## Sample Email Script

Dear Hiring Manager,

I understand that I was not offered the strategy manager position because Bellevue Consulting Group could not pay for my H-1B sponsorship. If that was the only reason I was not hired, I believe that we can brainstorm creative ways to cover sponsorship costs. If possible, I could cover some of the costs of getting the visa. I'm passionate about the company and the industry, so I'm willing to spend my own money to stay here and work. I don't have cash at the moment to pay upfront, but perhaps my portion of the payment for the sponsorship could be garnished from my wages. I'm very interested in working for you, so I hope that we can open up discussions about how we can make my employment work.

Thank you,

Jane

## Case 39: What to do if I want to enter the company at a higher level?

### Story

It's 2007, and Jane is interviewing with Microsoft. She finds out from an internal contact that the hiring manager has authority to hire a new candidate at either level 63 or 64. She wants to enter the organization at level 64, but she doesn't know how to convince the recruiter that she should be there.

What should she do?

### Solution

A disgruntled Microsoft employee released Microsoft's compensation table to the *Seattle Times*: http://bit.ly/MSFTComp.

It's from calendar year 2005, but it's still useful nonetheless. It indicates that following salary ranges:

**Microsoft Salary Table for Fiscal Year 2004**

| Level | Minimum | Midpoint | Maximum |
|-------|---------|----------|---------|
| 63 | $89,000 | $106,500 | $124,000 |
| 64 | $97,500 | $117,000 | $136,500 |

Source: *Seattle Times*

Most HR organizations update compensation tables each year to factor in cost of living increases. Looking at data from the US department of labor, cost of living has increased six percent in those two years. Adjusting the table for cost of living increases, here's the anticipated Microsoft salary table for 2006:

**Estimated Microsoft Salary Table for Fiscal Year 2006**

| Level | Minimum | Midpoint | Maximum |
|-------|---------|----------|---------|
| 63 | $94,340 | $112,890 | $131,440 |
| 64 | $103,350 | $124,020 | $144,690 |

Source: *Five Minutes to a Higher Salary*

To ensure a level of 64, request a base salary that's well beyond the level 63 designation. In this case, Jane should request a base salary of $137,000. That signals to the hiring manager that she's a level 64 candidate.

## Sample Person-to-Person Script

RECRUITER: How did your interviews go today?

JANE: It went well. I really enjoyed chatting with the team and learning more about the business. My favorite part of the day was seeing a demo for Microsoft PixelSense, the interactive table. I can see restaurants and hotels adopting the technology; it allow their guests to order food and play games while waiting.

RECRUITER: The team enjoyed meeting you too! Moving onto compensation, what is your expected salary?

JANE: I am expecting a base salary of around $137,000.

RECRUITER: $137,000 is a little higher than we budgeted for the position.

JANE: Well I'm sure that we could come to an agreement if we decide that I'm a good fit for the company. I'm willing to table compensation discussions until I get an offer from the company.

RECRUITER: That sounds fine. I'll keep your $137,000 expectation in mind.

*Three days later:*

RECRUITER: I'm pleased to present an offer to you today. Your title is Lead Program Manager, and your base salary is $137,000. You'll be eligible for an annual bonus of ten percent.

JANE: I'm really excited about the offer, and I'm glad you worked hard to make the $137,000 base salary work. I've got a follow-up question for you. What level is this role?

RECRUITER: This is a level 64 role.

JANE: Great! I'll accept now.

## Sample Email Script

Dear Recruiter,

Thank you for asking how my interview went. I think that the interview went very well. I really enjoyed chatting with the team and learning more about the business. My favorite part of the day was seeing a demo for Microsoft PixelSense, the interactive table. I can see restaurants and hotels adopting the technology; it allow their guests to order food and play games while waiting.

As to your question about expected salary, I am expecting a base salary of $137,000.

Thank you,

Jane

# Case 40: What should I do if I want a better job title?

## Story

Jane received a job offer to be a recruiter at a startup. While discussing the offer, the hiring manager informed her that she was going to be the only recruiter directly below the HR Director. The other recruiters were a few levels below her. Of course, Jane was pleasantly surprised, but wondered why she didn't have a better job title than the recruiters below her.

What should Jane do?

## Solution

Jane should ask for the desired job title during the negotiation process. It is an employee benefit that doesn't cost the company any money that could help advance her career.

## Sample Person-to-Person Script

JANE: May I ask you a few clarifying questions about the structure of the HR department?

HIRING MANAGER: Of course.

JANE: Will I be the only recruiter reporting directly to the HR Director?

HIRING MANAGER: That is correct.

JANE: Will the other recruiters report to me?

HIRING MANAGER: Yes.

JANE: Then can my title be changed from Senior Recruiting Manager to Group Recruiting Manager? My duties and compensation will not change at all. However, the title change is important to me. It indicates that I have managerial experience.

HIRING MANAGER: That seems fair. I'll discuss it with the CEO and see if we can formally change your title. Once we come to a decision, I'll contact you.

JANE: Great, thank you.

## Sample Email Script

Dear Hiring Manager,

Thank you for offering me the recruiter position at your company. I'm eager to join the team.

I do have a request. I was told that I will be the only recruiter reporting directly to the HR Director and that there are recruiters reporting to me. If so, can my title be changed from Senior Recruiting Manager to Group Recruiting Manager? My duties and compensation will not change at all. However, the title change is important to me. It indicates that I have managerial experience.

Thank you for your consideration. I look forward to hearing from you soon.

Sincerely,

Jane

## Case 41: How can I use mutual friends to get a better job offer?

### Story

Jane's manager wants to hire her to be a driver for his taxi cab company. She is new in town, but she and her manager have connections in common. Thanks to their shared ethnicity, the hiring manager knows Jane's aunts and uncles; all of them live in town.

He thinks she is talented, and she has the right experience. However, as part of the agreement, she has to rent his taxi cab for $300 per month and put down a $3,000 security deposit.

The problem: Jane doesn't have money for the security deposit.

She understands why the taxi cab owner demands a payment. It's not for regular wear-and-tear. Instead, some drivers abuse the taxis because it's not theirs.

What should Jane do?

### Solution

Instead of using a cash deposit as collateral, Jane can use her reputation instead. In many cultures, one's reputation is fiercely guarded. Since the boss knows her family very well, the boss can use Jane's family references to decide if he should give her the benefit of the doubt and allow her to work for him. If someone that her manager trusts is willing to vouch for her, then Jane's manager is more willing to give Jane a chance.

### Sample Person-to-Person Script

JANE: I would really like to accept the job, but I am not able to make the $3,000 security deposit. Would it be possible for us to find an alternative solution?

MANAGER: I'm willing to discuss options with you. Did you have anything in mind?

JANE: I know that you know my uncle very well and that you do business with him. Could you use a reference from him in place of a down payment?

MANAGER: Have you talked to him about this already?

JANE: Yes. He said that he's willing to vouch for me because he trusts me.

MANAGER: I'll talk to him about this then. I guess if he's willing to risk his reputation by recommending you, I can trust you without the deposit. I will call him tonight. If he agrees, you can have the job.

JANE: Thank you very much. You won't regret hiring me.

## Sample Email Script

Dear Manager,

Thank you for offering me the position. Since I'm new in town, it would give me a chance to make some money while I explore the city. I would like to accept the job, but I am not able to make the $3,000 security deposit.

I was hoping we could find an alternative solution. I know that you know my uncle very well and that you do business with him. Could you use a reference from him in place of a down payment? He said that he's willing to vouch for me.

I hope that we can come to a mutual agreement; I really want this position. I won't let you down.

Sincerely,

Jane

# Responding to a recruiter reaction

## Case 42: What should I do if the recruiter gives me a short deadline to accept the offer?

### Story

Jane just got an offer for a great position at a new company. However, Jane was immediately flooded with some mixed emotions; her recruiter gave her just one hour to decide. This was a big career move. Was the recruiter trying to pressure her?

Jane set aside her emotions for a moment. She's in the final stages of interviewing with another company, and Jane would like to hear their offer before making a decision.

What should Jane do?

### Solution

The one hour deadline may be a ploy to pressure Jane into accepting the offer. Many recruiters are evaluated based on the offer acceptance rate; that is, the number of candidate acceptances divided by the number of offers. For example, if the recruiter extends offers to 100 people and 95 of them accept, then the recruiter has an offer acceptance rate of 95 percent.

This is a critical recruiting metric because the company spends a lot of money and effort to find the right candidates. They don't want to lose them to other companies because of a weak closing process. To incentivize recruiters from closing candidates they like, many companies tie the recruiter's annual bonus to this metric.

To protect their offer acceptance rate, some recruiters use verbal offers to test a candidate's commitment to accepting the offer. If the candidate doesn't accept immediately, the candidate is written off as not receiving an official offer, and the rejection does not affect the recruiter's offer acceptance rate.

In this scenario, Jane should tell the recruiter how she is feeling. In addition, she can treat the hour deadline as a bluff from the recruiter and refuse to acknowledge it.

However, Jane must accept the consequence if the recruiter's threat is not a bluff. That is, if she doesn't accept within the hour, she might lose the offer. However, most recruiters would not enforce the one hour deadline. It's hard finding good candidates. Recruiters wouldn't risk losing an amazing employee just because the candidate needs extra time to consider the offer.

## Sample Person-to-Person Script

JANE: Thank you for offering me the position at your company, but I'm afraid I can't make a decision in one hour.

RECRUITER: Why not?

JANE: Well, I feel pressured to make a decision. My career is very important to me, and I need time to evaluate my options.

RECRUITER: You can't make the decision in an hour?

JANE: No, I can't. I am expecting another offer from another company. While I prefer this position, I have to evaluate both of them to make an informed decision. I can have a decision for you in a week.

RECRUITER: I have a lot of talented candidates in the pipeline, and we're one of the most desirable companies in the nation. I don't see why you're turning us down.

JANE: I'm not turning you down. I don't think it's wise for me to make a decision under pressure. I'd hate to be pressured into saying yes, join the company, and decide two weeks into the job that I made the wrong choice under the wrong conditions.

RECRUITER: Okay, that's fair. How much time do you need?

JANE: Can we set the deadline for one week from now?

RECRUITER: I can give you a week. But then I'm going to have to extend your offer to other candidates.

JANE: I understand. Thank you. I'll send you an email shortly to recap our conversation.

## Sample Email Script

Dear Recruiter,

Thank you for offering me the position at your company. I'm excited about the role, and I'm confident that I can bring a lot of value to your company.

However, I cannot make a decision whether to accept or reject the offer in an hour. I feel pressured to make a decision. My career is very important to me, so I do not want to be rushed into making a decision that could change my professional life. I am expecting an offer from another company, and while I would prefer this one, I need to evaluate both options to make an informed choice.

The earliest that I can make a decision is one week from now.

Thank you for considering my request,

Jane

## Case 43: What should I do if the company representative I'm talking to doesn't have any decision-making power?

### Story

Jane has recently been offered a new position with a starting base salary of $175,000. She thinks that she's worth at least another $25,000 and some other benefits, so she tries to negotiate with the recruiter. After a couple of days of difficult negotiations, the recruiter finally gives in and agrees to an extra $25,000. He tells Jane that she'll get the new offer in writing. However, when Jane actually receives the new offer, she sees that she only received a $10,000 increase. Jane calls the recruiter, and he tells her that he couldn't get his superiors to approve of the increase, so this was the best he could do. Jane is surprised because she assumed that the recruiter had the power to approve her requests.

What should Jane do?

### Solution

Jane should ask the recruiter who actually has decision-making power and speak directly with that person. It is less effective negotiating with someone who doesn't have the authority to approve requests.

In the future, Jane should ask from the beginning if the recruiter has decision-making power. If they say no, Jane should ask to speak directly with the person who does.

### Sample Person-to-Person Script

JANE: If you can't make decisions about my compensation, then who can?

RECRUITER: Well, my supervisor does. I need his approval to give you a salary increase.

JANE: Could I speak directly to him? It will save time and improve clarity in the negotiation process.

RECRUITER: You're actually supposed to negotiate with me.

JANE: I enjoy discussing salary with you, but I imagine you and your supervisor would like to get me on board as soon as possible. I feel the fastest way to do that is to negotiate directly with him.

*Recruiter pauses for a moment*

RECRUITER: Okay, I'll get you my boss' contact information.

*Jane then calls the HR Manager who has the power to make decisions about her compensation.*

JANE: Hello, my name is Jane. Is this the HR Manager?

HR MANAGER: Hello Jane. Yes, this is him.

JANE: The recruiter told me that you have decision-making power regarding my compensation. Is this true?

HR MANAGER: Yes it is. How can I help you?

JANE: Well the recruiter told me that she could approve my $25,000 increase in base salary, but when I received my new offer letter, I only received an extra $10,000. So I would like to discuss this with you and explain why I believe I'm worth the extra money.

HR MANAGER: Sure. Why don't you begin?

JANE: Thank you. To start, the market value of this position is $185,000 according to my contacts at your company. That means that the extra $10,000 only brought it up to the average salary of this position. However, I am more qualified than the average person in this position. To start, I received my undergraduate degree from Princeton and an MBA from Harvard, two distinguished schools. My prior experience is also more prestigious than most people in this position because of my previous experience at Goldman Sachs and McKinsey.

Not only did I work there, but I also was always ranked in the top 20% in every performance review.

HR MANAGER: I see. You certainly are more qualified. Well, we would really like you on board. I'll approve your original request so that your base salary will be $200,000.

JANE: Thank you. I'm glad we could come to an agreement. I'm confident that I can bring a lot of value to your organization.

## Sample Email Script

Dear HR Manager,

My name is Jane, and I was recently offered a position at your company. I would like to thank you for offering me the job.

During negotiations, the recruiter told me that he could approve my $25,000 increase in base salary. I thought it was a done deal, but when I received my new offer letter, I only received an extra $10,000. So I would like to discuss this with you. I believe I'm worth the extra money, and I'd to explain why.

To start, the market value of this position is $185,000 according to my contacts in the organization. That means that the extra $10,000 only brought it up to the average salary of this position. However, I am more qualified than the average person in this position. To start, I received my undergraduate degree from Princeton and an MBA from Harvard, two distinguished schools. My prior experience is also more prestigious than most people in this position because of my previous roles at Goldman Sachs and McKinsey. Not only did I work there, but I also was always ranked in the top 20% in every performance review.

That's why I am requesting $200,000 in base salary. I believe that this would be fair compensation for the position and my qualifications.

I'm eager to accept, and I hope that we can come to an agreement. I'm confident that I can add a lot of value to the organization.

Thank you,

Jane

# Case 44: What should I do if a recruiter pulls an offer?

## Story

Jane received a $60,000 offer. Jane told the recruiter that the salary was low and that she expected to get something closer to $80,000.

The recruiter then mumbles that $80,000 is doable. Jane then asks the recruiter to ask his manager to see if "they could offer more (than the $80,000)."

After ending the conversation, the recruiter calls in five minutes and tells Jane that the $80,000 offer is a mistake. The only offer that's being made is an offer for $60,000.

At that point, Jane gets angry at the recruiter for revoking the verbal offer. Jane then rejects the $60,000 offer.

What should Jane do now?

## Solution

### What the Candidate Needs to Do Now

The recruiter pulled the $80,000 offer because Jane came across as hard to please. When candidates come across as difficult, the recruiter is not going to do any favors. Most recruiters have their personal pride; many will not be steamrolled by a demanding candidate.

At this point, Jane needs to apologize for rejecting the offer brusquely. From there, she should politely ask if $80,000 base salary offer is available and ask what she needs to do to be eligible for it.

### What the Candidate Needs to Do in the Future

Jane's problem was that she couldn't quit while she was ahead and that was because she didn't know that she was ahead. In other words, she failed to set the minimum salary she was willing to accept, which we call the reservation price. Related to the reservation price is Jane's BATNA, or best alternative to a negotiated agreement. Jane, at this point, did not have any other offers.

Next, recruiters expect candidates to honor a promise. In this case, the recruiter felt he did his job. That is, get the $80,000 base salary that the candidate requested. Now, the recruiter is expecting the candidate to reciprocate and accept. When the candidate did not do as expected, the recruiter retaliated by pulling the offer from the table.

Does this mean that the candidate won't get a salary offer above $80,000? Not at all. The candidate can make a request for a salary that's higher than $80,000. However, the request must accompany a new piece of information or some other justification. For example, if the candidate recently received an offer from another firm that's paying more, that could be grounds for requesting more than $80,000.

## Sample Person-to-Person Script

*Jane calls the recruiter a couple hours after she rejected the company's $60,000 offer*

JANE: I wanted to apologize for how our last conversation ended. I was angry when I heard that the $80,000 offer was no longer on the table. It felt as if the company did not believe I was worth $80,000.

RECRUITER: Thank you for your apology.

JANE: Can you explain to what happened?

RECRUITER: What do you mean?

JANE: I'd like to understand why you pulled the $80,000 offer after you told me that it was doable.

RECRUITER: After you told me that you "wanted more," I discussed your request with the hiring manager. We felt that you were hard to please, and we were concerned about bidding against ourselves in this negotiation. We looked at your background, and we genuinely thought, with the information we have now about your contribution, you would be worth roughly $60,000.

JANE: That's fair. You and the hiring manager haven't seen me perform on the job. I have a question for you. What would it have taken for us to reach an agreement?

RECRUITER: We'd like you to accept the $60,000. However, we do understand that you feel that you're worth $80,000. The hiring manager would be comfortable doing an accelerated three month review of your salary. If you've proven that you can add significant value, we'd be happy to raise your salary to $80,000 at that time.

JANE: You can imagine I would have loved to have receive $80,000 outright. However, I see from your standpoint that I haven't quite proven myself. If you can write in the $80,000 base salary, contingent on a successful performance review into the offer, then I'll accept it today.

RECRUITER: Sounds good. I'll send you the revised offer shortly.

## Sample Email Script

Dear Recruiter,

I wanted to apologize for how our last conversation ended. I was upset when I heard that the $80,000 offer was no longer on the table. It felt as if the company did not believe I was worth $80,000.

I'd like to understand why you decided to pull the $80,000 offer after you told me that it was doable. I'm still very interested in the position, and I am hoping that we could open the discussion again.

Thank you,

Jane

# Negotiating a raise

## Case 45: What should I do if I'm scared to ask my boss for a raise?

### Story

Jane has worked for her employer for three years since she became a Certified Public Accountant. She would like to ask for a raise, but she's unsure how to approach it. As an accountant, she doesn't have a lot of experience negotiating. She feels awkward about the situation and would much rather not confront her manager about it because she likes working at the company.

What should Jane do?

### Solution

Jane's fear is completely normal. In fact, a lot of people are uncomfortable with confrontation because they're afraid they will damage their relationship, get rejected, or worse: get fired. However, a recent Salary.com survey announced that zero percent of employers have demoted or fired an employee after they asked for a raise. While that does not mean that it has never happened or never will happen, it seems unlikely. To ask for a raise, Jane needs to tell herself that it is okay to ask for a raise.

Given this reality, it is important for Jane to speak up. Jane needs to understand that her manager is not a mind reader. If she doesn't ask for what she wants, her manager won't know and can't give it to her.

If Jane hopes that her manager will magically read her mind, she'll be disappointed when she doesn't get what she wants. It'll stir resentment and bring misery. It's Jane's career, not her manager's career. She has to speak up if she wants something.

To prepare, Jane should practice negotiating with friends and family. This way she can get more comfortable with negotiating. Jane should also prepare a list of talking points to back up her case; knowing what she's going to say will help her feel more confident.

## Sample Person-to-Person Script

JANE: Hello, do you have a moment? I would like to discuss something with you.

MANAGER: Of course. What can I do for you?

JANE: I would like to request a raise.

*Her manager sounds surprised.*

MANAGER: Okay, we can talk about that. How much are you looking for?

JANE: I would like an eight percent raise.

MANAGER: That seems a little high. Why do you think you deserve that?

*Jane gets a little nervous at this point, but continues the conversation because she realizes that his question is not a rejection. He just needs justification that she deserves it.*

JANE: I have been working here for three years. Since then, I haven't received a raise. I feel that the value I bring to the company merits a raise.

For instance, I uncovered financial irregularities in our reports, which led to the collection of over one million dollars in overdue account receivables. I was also the primary advisor for our most recent land acquisition, saving us $58,000 by identifying new concessions.

MANAGER: You have done a lot to help the company reach its goals. I recently learned that the $58,000 you saved from the land acquisition funded the newly approved Silver Valley mall project, which has a lot of potential to drive new revenue.

*Jane remains silent, waiting until she gets a firmer answer from her manager.*

MANAGER: Let me ask my boss. I think I can get you that eight percent raise. You deserve it.

JANE: Thank you. I really appreciate it.

## Sample Email Script

Dear Manager,

As you know, I have been working here for three years. Since then, I haven't received a raise, but I feel that I have demonstrated value for the company that merits a raise.

For instance, I uncovered financial irregularities in our reports, which led to the collection of over one million dollars in overdue account receivables. I was also the primary advisor for our most recent land acquisition, saving us $58,000 by identifying new concessions.

I enjoy working at the company and with this team. I hope that we can come to a mutual agreement.

Thank you,

Jane

## Case 46: What should I do if I'm being paid under market value?

### Story

Jane has been working at her current company for one year. When she joined the company, she had been unemployed for two years, primarily to spend more time with her family. Since she really wanted to join, she accepted the company's offer even though friends told her it was 20 percent lower than the market average.

The company's financial performance improved shortly after a new product launch, and the company raised a new round of funding. She had been a top performer at the company during the year and was hoping for a large raise. Her annual review is approaching soon and Jane wants to ask for a big salary increase to account for her low initial salary and her above average performance.

How should she ask?

### Solution

It's a great time to ask for a raise while the company is doing well financially. It sounds like the company is aware that Jane's current salary is low given her excellent performance and recent salary data in the industry. The company is likely to give her a raise. After all, she is a top performer and a valuable employee that they want to keep.

Jane can also use precise numbers to get what she wants. She knows that her salary is about twenty percent below market value, but a round number like "20 percent" sounds like an arbitrary estimate. She will increase her credibility if she asks for a more specific increase in her salary, such as "22 percent" or "24 percent". If Jane uses precise numbers, it will seem like she did her research to come up with that number.

### Sample Person-to-Person Script

JANE: I would like to request a raise. I'm currently being paid under market value.

MANAGER: We were thinking that you deserved a raise too. We had planned a 15 percent raise for you; it's higher that what we had planned for your peers.

JANE: Thank you. I would like to discuss how I can get a bigger raise. When I first joined this company, I was being paid 20 percent below the industry average. I knew that the company was going through a financial hardship, so I accepted a lower offer. Now that the company is doing well again, I would like to raise my salary to be in-line with market averages.

MANAGER: That sounds pretty reasonable. How much are you requesting?

JANE: Actually, I would like to ask for 23 percent; that would bump me up to $107,500, which is the industry median for someone in my role.

MANAGER: I think we can do 23 percent. Let me check with the HR department, and I'll get back to you.

JANE: Thanks for considering my request. I look forward to hearing from you soon.

## Sample Email Script

Dear Manager,

As you know, I joined the team a year ago when the company was facing financial troubles. Because I was passionate about the opportunity, I joined with a very low starting salary. Now that the company is doing well again, I would like to request a raise. When I joined, I was paid 20 percent below market value.

I have recently researched median salaries for my role, and it is now at $107,500. That's a 23 percent increase. I would like to get that market level adjustment.

I am confident that I am worth the raise. I look forward to hearing from you soon.

Thank you,

Jane

## Case 47: What should I do if new employees are making more than me?

### Story

In 2004, with a newly minted MBA from a top-tier school, Jane joined a Fortune 500 company with an $85,000 salary. She received a standard three percent increase every year.

| | '04 Cohort | '05 Cohort | '06 Cohort | '07 Cohort | '08 Cohort |
|---|---|---|---|---|---|
| Base Salary | $85,000 | $90,000 | $95,000 | $100,000 | $105,000 |
| % Annual Increase | 3% | 3% | 3% | 3% | 3% |

Five years later, in 2008, she's no longer happy with her salary. With her standard three percent raise, Jane is now making $95,668 per year. The latest MBAs are making $105,000 per year, so she's making roughly $10,000 less than they are.

| | '04 Cohort | '05 Cohort | '06 Cohort | '07 Cohort | '08 Cohort |
|---|---|---|---|---|---|
| 2004 | $85,000 | | | | |
| 2005 | $87,550 | $90,000 | | | |
| 2006 | $90,177 | $92,700 | $95,000 | | |
| 2007 | $92,882 | $95,481 | $97,850 | $100,000 | |
| 2008 | $95,668 | $98,345 | $100,786 | $103,000 | $105,000 |

Enough is enough. She wants a raise.

### Solution

Jane should ask her manager for a market adjustment. If she were a new MBA today, she would start off with $105,000 base salary. She should use this as the new baseline for what would be equivalent pay with today's market conditions.

With five years of service, she would get five annual increases of three percent each. Compounding that growth, Jane would get $105,000 * (1 + 3%) ^ 5 = $121,724.

That's a $26,056 raise from the $95,668 she's making today!

## Sample Person-to-Person Script

JANE: I'd like to request a raise.

*Her manager shifts uncomfortably*

MANAGER: Why are you looking for a raise?

JANE: I've been working at the company for five years. I've noticed that the new MBAs are getting bigger and better offers. In fact, the new MBAs are now making $105,000 straight from school. I'm making approximately $95,000. That's almost $10,000 less for someone who has significantly more experience and a proven track record.

MANAGER: I agree that your salary hasn't kept up with what we're currently paying new MBA grads. How much of a raise are you looking for?

JANE: I'm requesting a new base salary of $121,724.

MANAGER: How did you arrive at that number?

JANE: I'm looking for a market adjustment that's in-line with what new grads are getting now, which is $105,000. I've also factored in the three percent annual increase I've received each year based on my solid performance and contribution to the team and business. I'll email you my calculations right now.

*Jane emails her boss the aforementioned calculations, including the following equation:*

*$105,000 * (1 + 3%) ^ 5 = $121,724*

MANAGER: Your logic is sound. Our next review cycle is two months from now, but I will bring your request for a market-adjustment to our HR and compensation team. Given your strong performance and loyal service to the company, I'll fight hard for your raise.

JANE: Thanks.

*Three months from now, her manager announces that they've not only given Jane a market adjustment, but they've also given her a promotion which comes with a new title.*

## Sample Email Script

Dear Manager,

As we approach the end of the year, I would like to discuss my compensation with you. I've been working at the company for five years, and I've noticed that the new MBAs are getting bigger and bigger offers. In fact, the new MBAs are now making $105,000 straight from school. I'm making approximately $95,000. That's almost $10,000 less for someone who has significantly more work experience and a proven track record at the company.

That's why I would like to request a new base salary of $121,724. I'm looking for a market adjustment that's in-line with what new grads are getting now, which is $105,000. I've also factored in the three percent annual increase I've received each year based on my solid performance and contribution to the team and business.

I arrived at my request based on this equation: $105,000 * (1 + 3\%) \wedge 5 = \$121,724$

I really enjoy working here and that this company values its employees, so I hope you will consider my request. I'm confident that I can keep adding value to the company.

Thank you,

Jane

## Case 48: What should I do if my colleagues make more money than me?

### Story

Jane started her career at a small San Francisco start-up in 2012, making $45,000 as an account manager. Two years later, she found that her colleagues are making $70,000. To get a fair salary, she is thinking about asking for a $25,000 raise, which will bring her salary to $70,000.

What should Jane do?

### Solution

Jane should definitely ask for a raise. What she needs to do is explain to her manager why she deserves a new raise. That includes her contributions to the company and how she will continue to be worth that raise in the future.

### Sample Person-to-Person Script

JANE: In our one-on-one today, there are two things I'd like to cover: my request for a raise and my plan on how I plan on earning it. I'd like to first summarize my key accomplishments. I manage a $728,000 book of business and grew revenue from $392,000 to $728,000 over the last two years. I increased the video advertising revenue mix from 5 percent to 50 percent over the last two years as well. I also trained and mentored 10 new junior account managers in the last year alone.

MANAGER: That is impressive. How much are you asking for?

JANE: I'm currently making $45,000. My research indicates that, given my accomplishments, I am being underpaid. The market value for my accomplishments is $70,000.

MANAGER: That sounds fair. You mentioned that you also had plans for earning the raise in the future?

JANE: Yes. Here's my plan on how I intend to earn my raise over the next three months. I plan to have more face-to-face time with our clients by visiting them once a week, doing monthly skip level meetings, and performing a quarterly audit. I'll also run my own weekly brown bag training sessions. The topics will cover prospecting, relationship management, and time management.

MANAGER: That seems ambitious. Are you sure that those goals can be completed in a timely manner without sacrificing your current responsibilities?

JANE: Of course. I love what I do, and I don't mind putting in the extra hours.

MANAGER: I love your ambition. Give me a couple of days to touch base with the CEO and our VP of Human Resources. Once I get an answer, I'll let you know.

JANE: Thank you for your time.

## Sample Email Script

Dear Manager,

As we approach the end of the year and performance reviews, I would like to ask for a raise.

I'd like to first summarize my key accomplishments. I manage a $728,000 book of business and grew revenue from $392,000 to $728,000 over the last two years. I increased the video advertising revenue mix from 5 percent to 50 percent over the last two years as well. I also trained and mentored 10 new junior account managers in the last year alone.

I'm currently making $45,000, but my research indicates that my market value is really $70,000. That is the new salary I'm looking for.

I have also created a plan on how I intend to earn my raise over the next three months. I plan to have more face-to-face time with our clients by visiting them once a week, taking monthly skip levels, and performing a quarterly audit. I'll also run my own weekly brown bag training sessions. The topics will cover prospecting, relationship management, and time efficiency.

I'm confident that we can come to an agreement and that I can continue to bring value to our organization.

Thank you,

Jane

# Case 49: What should I do if no one else asks for a raise?

## Story

Jane has worked at her current company for two years and believes that she deserves a raise. However, she doesn't think that any of her coworkers have asked for a raise from her boss and assumes that there is a good reason. After all, her coworkers have worked at the company longer than she has; they must know something about the lack of raises that she doesn't. Suffering through a gut-wrenching process that flip flops between desire and doubt, she's leaning toward passing on her raise ask.

What should Jane do?

## Solution

Salary.com surveyed 1,000 employees and found that raises are indeed quite common. 58 percent of respondents received a raise in the current year. The number increases to 76 percent in the last two years, and 88 percent in the last three years.

The same survey indicates that people requested a 16 percent raise, but received a nine percent raise. The average dollar amount of raises is $3,334.

The data shows that a lot of people are getting raises. Most of these people probably asked for them too. The best person to advocate for Jane's pay is Jane herself. She should speak up. For the sake of privacy, it is also common to not reveal pay and pay raises, so Jane might have just not heard about the raises that were given.

## Sample Person-to-Person Script

JANE: I would like to request a raise.

MANAGER: Why are you looking for a raise?

JANE: I have been working at the company for two years, and I have helped the company reach its goals. I completed my portion of the Guardian Project long before the deadline and was a major player of the Rainier Valley acquisition for our department. I also took over half of James' role while he was on paternity leave.

MANAGER: Yes, you've really stepped up for the company, especially in the last year. How much are you asking for?

*Jane is surprised that he isn't resisting a raise.*

JANE: I would like a seven percent raise.

*Jane's manager thinks about it for a few seconds.*

MANAGER: That makes sense. Okay, I'll send your seven percent request up to HR.

JANE: Thank you. I really appreciate it.

## Sample Email Script

Dear Manager,

Before we approach the end of the year, I would like to discuss my compensation with you.

In short, I would like to request a raise of seven percent because I have helped the company reach its goals. I completed my portion of the Guardian Project long before the deadline and was a major player of the Rainier Valley acquisition for our department. I also took over half of James' role while he was on paternity leave.

Thanks for reviewing my request. I'd be happy to discuss in more detail and provide more information.

Thank you,

Jane

# Case 50: What should I do if I want a raise for a valuable contribution I made to the company?

## Story

Jane has been working at her current position for only a year, but she has already exceeded expectations. She landed several multi-million dollar contracts with top brands and impressed her managers with her personality and attention to detail.

Despite her inexperience, Jane's top-tier education vaulted her starting salary into the top half of the pay scale with $104,000. Given her exceptional performance, Jane believes she is underpaid. She knows that the company needs her to retain these clients, yet she doesn't want to threaten the company with quitting because she enjoys her job.

What should Jane do?

## Solution

Jane is right. She shouldn't threaten to leave the company, even if it may get her a raise. It could negatively affect her professional relationships and impact her reputation.

Jane has impressed her managers, and they know how valuable she is. Her managers will be willing to negotiate with Jane to keep her satisfied.

Since she's already at the top half of her pay level, Jane should request a raise and a promotion into the new grade level.

## Sample Person-to-Person Script

JANE: I would like to request a raise.

MANAGER: Okay, I'm listening.

JANE: Here's why I'm asking for a raise: I'm bringing more value to the company. In the last year, I landed several new clients worth $75 million in incremental annual sales.

MANAGER: Yes, I'm definitely aware of your accomplishments, and thank you for reminding me. What kind of a raise did you have in mind?

JANE: Since I'm at the top end of my pay level, I would like to get promoted to the next grade level.

MANAGER: The next grade level starts at $100,000, which is $4,000 less than what you're marking currently. Is there anything else you're asking for?

JANE: In addition to the level bump, I'd like to get a $6,000 increase in base salary from $104,000 to $110,000.

MANAGER: I think we can agree to that. You have convinced me that you deserve a big raise. I'll send this request up to my boss and HR. I'll keep you posted on what they say.

JANE: Thank you. I really appreciate it.

## Sample Email Script

Dear Manager,

I am requesting a promotion into a new level, along with a salary raise from $104,000 to $110,000.

Here's why I feel I deserve the raise: I'm bringing more value to the company. In the last year, I landed several new clients worth $75 million in incremental annual sales.

Since I'm at the top end of my pay level, I would like to get promoted to the next grade level. In addition, I'd like to get a $6,000 increase in base salary from $104,000 to $110,000.

Thanks for considering my request. I'd be happy to discuss in more detail and provide more information.

Thank you,

Jane

## Case 51: What should I do if I need a cost of living adjustment because of a transfer?

### Story

Jane is being transferred from Austin, Texas to Seattle, Washington to lead the Pacific Northwest branch of her company. Jane found that the cost of living in Seattle is much higher than Austin's, but her salary will not change to adjust for the cost of living difference. She wants to move to Seattle and thinks it will be a good opportunity for her, but she doesn't want her living standard to change.

What should Jane do?

### Solution

Jane should ask for a cost of living adjustment, also known by the acronym COLA, to account for the differences between prices in Austin and Seattle. If Jane's salary remains stagnant, her standard of living will actually fall because she will have less purchasing power with the same salary.

Jane should research how much the cost of living in Seattle compares to Austin. If Jane has concrete evidence that the change in the cost of living will be significant, then her manager is more likely to approve her request.

### Sample Person-to-Person Script

JANE: Thank you for offering me the position in Seattle. I'm excited to join a new team in the company.

HIRING MANAGER: You're welcome. We're excited to have you here in Seattle.

JANE: Thank you. I would like to discuss my compensation with you. I don't see any sign that my compensation is going to change, but the cost of living in Seattle is much greater than here in Austin. That is why I would like to request a cost of living adjustment to relocate to Seattle.

MANAGER: I see. How much are you asking for?

JANE: Well, Seattle has about a 25 percent higher cost of living than Austin. To maintain my standard of living, my $150K salary will have to rise to $190K.

MANAGER: A $40K increase is a lot. I don't think that will get approved.

JANE: It is important to me. Can you ask your boss for me?

MANAGER: Ok, I'll give it a shot.

JANE: Thanks!

## Sample Email Script

Dear Manager,

I'm excited to relocate and be part of the Pacific Northwest team in Seattle.

Before I accept however, I would like to discuss my compensation package. Seattle has a much higher cost of living than Austin. Will my compensation be adjusted for the higher cost of living?

My research indicates that Seattle has about a 25 percent higher cost of living than Austin. That means that my current $150K salary is not worth as much in Seattle. To maintain my same standard of living, I will need approximately $190K in Seattle.

Thanks for considering my request. I look forward to hearing from you soon.

Thank you,

Jane

## Case 52: What should I do after a probation period in my new job?

### Story

Jane just graduated from college and received a job offer for her first full time job. Jane believed that she deserved a five percent increase in her base salary, but her hiring manager was not sure. To prove her worth, Jane negotiated for a probationary period of six months. After six months, she would receive an early review and hopefully a five percent raise. The end of her probation period is approaching. Jane is not clear that the review will be scheduled.

What should Jane do?

### Solution

Jane should approach her manager and ask to schedule the early review to a date either on or very near the six month deadline. Jane should also prepare for her early review by making a list of accomplishments. She can also detail ideas and future work to help the company.

To prepare, use Resources D and E in the Appendix. Resource D, the candidate side worksheet, will supply your boss with the talking points they need to fight for your raise or promotion.

Resource E provides three examples of performance review sheets. Your company will likely have their own performance review template, but I have included these as reference.

### Sample Person-to-Person Script

JANE: Are you ready to discuss my performance-to-date and my salary review?

MANAGER: Yes I am.

JANE: I want to start by saying thank you for the opportunity. I have really enjoyed my time here, and I can't wait to talk about the progress I've made.

MANAGER: I'm glad you enjoy it here. We appreciate your work too.

JANE: Thank you. To begin, I'll start by listing my accomplishments in those six months. You asked me to achieve the $1.3 MM quota for the Midwest region, and I exceeded that goal by $200k.

You also challenged me to take a leadership role and mentor others. I took on several one-on-one meetings to mentor junior employees. I also shared my personal best practices in a 300 person presentation called Social Media Best Practices for Sales People. I received an 8.9 out of 10 on post-event surveys.

MANAGER: Yes, I was quite pleased about how you exceed sales goals. Several people have told me that your presentation went well.

JANE: Thank you. To show that I'm committed to the company, I've thought about some new ideas to help the company. I'd like to build a new sales tool called the Enterprise Configurator. I believe it'll accelerate our sales velocity and augment next quarter's revenues by 15%.

MANAGER: That's quite ambitious. Are you sure that can be done?

JANE: Yes. I talked to the marketing team last week. I presented my proposal for the Enterprise Configurator. After some good collaboration, they decided to make it one of their top three priorities. Partnering together, we can accomplish this quickly and get this launched by next quarter.

MANAGER: Sounds good.

JANE: I would like to now discuss my compensation with you. Since I have demonstrated my value during the first six months, I would like to request a salary increase of five percent.

MANAGER: Five percent... I think we can do that. You certainly were a top performer despite being new. I'll send this request to HR after the meeting.

JANE: Thank you. I really appreciate you allowing me to have an early review.

## Sample Email Script

Dear Hiring Manager,

Thanks for hearing out my request for a raise.

I want to start by saying thank you for the opportunity. I have really enjoyed my time here, and I can't wait to talk about the progress I've made.

To begin, I'll start by listing my accomplishments in my first six months. You asked me to achieve the $1.3 MM quota for the Midwest region, and I exceeded that goal by $200k.

You also challenged me to take a leadership role and mentor others. I took on several one-on-one meetings to mentor junior employees. I also shared my personal best practices in a 300 person presentation called Social Media Best Practices for Sales People. I received an 8.9 out of 10 on post-event surveys.

To show that I'm committed to the company, I've thought about some new ideas to help the company. My favorite idea is a new sales tool called the Enterprise Configurator. I think it will accelerate our sales velocity and augment next quarter's revenues by approximately 15%. The marketing department is on board, and they've made it one of their top priorities.

Given my performance, I feel I've earned a raise. As a result, I would like to request a salary increase of five percent.

Thanks for your consideration, and I look forward to hearing from you soon.

Thank you,

Jane

## Case 53: What should I do if I want a raise, but I just get a compliment and a pat on the back?

### Story

Jane is a top performing employee at her current company. In her performance reviews, she has always been rated in the top 20% of her peer group, ever since she started two years ago.

When she asked for a raise six months ago, her manager avoided the discussion and gave her empty praise. He appreciates her contribution, but he has not demonstrated his appreciation with any rewards.

Jane is ready to ask for the raise once more. This time, Jane wants to be prepared in case he just gives her a pat on the back again.

What should Jane do?

### Solution

When her boss tries to deviate from the topic, Jane should re-direct the conversation back to her promotion request. Jane should not give up when her manager tries to change the subject.

If she feels like the boss is wasting her time, Jane can put her foot down, end the unproductive conversation, and resume the discussion later.

For those who aren't comfortable with confrontation, this may seem very bold. However, standing your ground may be necessary; otherwise the other party may exploit your lack of resolve to not give what you want.

### Sample Person-to-Person Script

JANE: I'd like to discuss a salary increase.

MANAGER: You're a treasured asset to our organization. We really appreciate everything you do for us. Are you looking for a juicier assignment? We need a talented marketer to represent us in Cannes, France next week. Want to go?

JANE: That sounds interesting. But I want a salary increase.

MANAGER: How about we give you an extra two days off during this long weekend? No need to report it. You've earned it.

JANE: I feel like you're avoiding the issue.

MANAGER: Not at all. I'm just trying to show how much I appreciate you.

JANE: I feel like you don't want to discuss a salary increase. In our current conversation, every time I bring the salary increase up, I perceive that you are trying to change the topic. It feels like you're avoiding my request.

MANAGER: Well, I'm not avoiding. And I do value your contribution.

JANE: The salary increase discussion is important to me. If you're not prepared to have the discussion now, I can leave, so you can collect your thoughts. I'll look for time on your calendar later this week to resume the discussion.

## Sample Email Script

Dear Manager,

As I mentioned before, I would like to request a raise. I found it difficult to discuss it with you in person, so I would like to put my request in writing with this email.

I would like a six percent raise. Since I joined the company two years ago, I've been consistently rated in the top 20% of my peer group. You asked me to achieve the $1.3 MM quota for the Midwest region, and I exceeded that goal by $200k.

You also asked me to be more visible in our department, especially with the newer employees. I stepped up to the challenge by mentoring them one-on-one. I also presented Social Media Best Practices for Sales People to over 300 attendees; I received an 8.9 out of 10 on post-event surveys.

This is why I feel I deserve a raise. If you disagree, that is fine by me, but I would like to understand why.

Thank you,

Jane

# Case 54: What to do if I want more vacation days this year?

## Story

In the last six months, Jane had to assume duties of another colleague who was fired earlier in the year. They hired a replacement just last week.

Jane is feeling burnt out. Her workload increased an additional 15 hours per week during this time period. She would like to have some time off.

What should she do?

## Solution

Most managers do not have to ask HR or their boss to approve extra vacation days, especially for a valued employee. As a result, extra vacation days is one of the easier perks to obtain.

Jane is more likely to get her vacation request granted if Jane can frame the vacation as a benefit to the company.

## Sample Person-to-Person Script

JANE: I would like to request six more paid vacation days this year because of the extra work I had to do after Matt was let go.

MANAGER: Can you explain a little more?

JANE: After Matt departed the company, I had to pick up his book of business. He was responsible for over 20 clients, including some of the most demanding clients in our department. It took us six months to hire Matt's backfill. During that time, I had to work an extra 15 hours per week to service Matt's clients.

It was an exhausting time, but I'm proud to say that his client list is better now than it was six months ago. Revenue has increased 15%

year-over-year. In the annual client survey, our net promoter score increased 500 basis points year-over-year.

When the company was restructuring, Matt was laid off. He had open sales accounts with a lot of clients, so I had to take over those accounts in addition to my own. So for the last six months, I had to work 60 hour weeks to get everything done.

MANAGER: We feel really bad about having Matt's role vacant for so long. We appreciate you filling in for him, and we're thrilled to see the remarkable improvement in his accounts. I imagine you're ready to catch your breath.

JANE: You're welcome. But yes, I do feel burnt out, and I miss my family. I need to take some time off to relax and spend time with my husband and kids. I know that when I return I'll be re-energized and ready to perform at my best again.

MANAGER: Do you have any dates you want to propose?

JANE: I'd like to use the extra vacation right after I transition Matt's accounts to the new hire.

MANAGER: That sounds reasonable. Your request is approved. Thank you for your hard work this year.

JANE: Thank you very much.

## Sample Email Script

Dear Manager,

I would like to request six extra vacation days this year. After Matt departed the company, I had to pick up his book of business. During that time, I had to work an extra 15 hours per week to service Matt's clients.

It was an exhausting time, but I'm proud to say that his client list is better now than it was six months ago. Revenue has increased 15%

year-over-year. In the annual client survey, our net promoter score increased 500 basis points year-over-year.

Now I feel burnt out, and I miss my family. I need to take some time off to relax and spend time with my husband and kids. When I return, I'll be re-energized and ready to perform at my best again.

I'd like to use the extra vacation right after I transition Matt's accounts to the new hire.

Thanks for considering my request,

Jane

# Negotiating other issues

## Case 55: What should I do if I need a career break?

### Story

Jane has been working at her current company for ten years. She feels burnt out and would like to take time off to finish writing a book that she started three years ago. However, her job only gives her three vacation weeks, and she doesn't feel it would be enough time to complete it. She wants to take a break from her career for a few months, but doesn't want to quit her job either.

What should she do?

### Solution

Jane should negotiate for a sabbatical. A sabbatical is not just a long vacation. Instead, it is a paid leave meant to be used in a productive way such as study or travel. In Jane's case, she would use her sabbatical to complete her book. A sabbatical can be as short as a few months to as long as a few years. It depends on how much time one needs and how much time your employer is willing to give. Jane should emphasize that she doesn't want to quit, but instead take a short career break.

### Sample Person-to-Person Script

JANE: I would like to request a sabbatical. I have been working at the company for ten years, and I feel burnt out. I would like some time to recharge.

MANAGER: I see. Can't we just give you an extra week of vacation?

JANE: I appreciate the offer, but I was thinking closer to five months. I would like to take the time to finish a book that I have been writing.

MANAGER: Unfortunately, we do not have budget to cover a paid sabbatical. And five months is quite a long time. Who would fill in for you while you are away?

JANE: Once our new product launches, I think that would be a great time to do the sabbatical. It'll naturally wrap-up my responsibility as launch lead. As for the cost concerns, I'm willing to take an unpaid sabbatical, but I do ask that my dental and health insurance continue to be covered during this period.

MANAGER: If you can convince your sister teams to pick up the work and responsibility for the upcoming sustain-and-maintain marketing plan, then I'll go to HR with your request.

JANE: That sounds reasonable.

## Sample Email Script

Dear Manager,

As you know, I have been working at the company for ten years. I feel burnt out and would like to request a sabbatical to recharge. I would like a five month break; I would use the sabbatical to finish a book that I have been writing.

I would like to emphasize however that I'm not quitting. I understand that the sabbatical will probably be unpaid, but I want to return to my position. However, I would like to continue to be covered under the corporate health and dental plans during my sabbatical.

I'd like to take the sabbatical after the new product launches, so that there's no disruption to our current work. Understandably, you might be concerned on who would pick up the work for our sustain-and-maintain marketing efforts while I'm away. I've talked to our sister teams, and they're open to picking up this work on our team's behalf.

I'd be happy to answer any questions you may have, and thanks for considering my request.

Thank you,

Jane

## Case 56: What should I do if I want to request flexible working hours?

### Story

Jane is requesting flexible work hours so that she can pick up her kids from day care. She wants to work a full day but would like to shift her schedule around. Her workplace doesn't require constant personal communication, so Jane thought that transferring to a more flexible work schedule would be easy to accommodate. However, when she approached her manager, he was not supportive and demeaning.

What should she do?

### Solution

Most employers understand the need for flexible work schedules and its impact on employee morale, especially with today's dual career families. However, most employers are worried flexible work schedules will impact individual and team productivity. Convince your boss or employer that overall productivity will stay the same or increase, and you'll likely get the flexible work schedule you desire.

### Sample Person-to-Person Script

JANE: I know the company's employees usually don't come in until 9 a.m., but I would prefer if I could start my work day at 6 a.m. and end at 3 p.m.

MANAGER: Oh there's no need. You have to get home to the kids. Just come in at 9 a.m., and you're free to skip meetings after 3 p.m. Just send me your notes and action items if you have issues to raise.

JANE: You're okay with that?

MANAGER: Nope. You've got mommy duty.

JANE: You don't need me here? So much for the women's liberation movement.

MANAGER: Wow, I thought you'd be more grateful.

JANE: Well, I wasn't asking to skip the meeting. I was asking to have a full work day, but start earlier in the day.

MANAGER: Alright, you're right. I missed your initial request. I don't see any problems with you having an earlier workday as long as your co-workers are okay with it.

## Sample Email Script

Dear Manager,

I know the company's employees usually don't come in until 9 a.m., but I would prefer if I could start my work day at 6 a.m. and end at 3 p.m. I would still work the full nine hours, but I would like to leave earlier so I can pick up my kids from school.

I imagine you're concerned on the impact on my productivity. I'll be available on my smartphone to take care of any issues that transpired when I was away from the office. I'll tell the team that they shouldn't hesitate to reach out to me, even if it's late at night.

If we need to meet face-to-face, I would just ask the team to meet with me earlier in the day. If that creates an issue, I can make arrangements with my husband, on an as-needed basis, to pick up the kids for the day.

Thank you,

Jane

## Case 57: What should I do if I have an upcoming performance review?

### Story

Jane, a new college graduate, is approaching her first performance review ever. She's not sure what to expect or how to prepare for it.

There is one thing for certain; she wants a bonus to cover some unexpected medical bills.

What should Jane do?

### Solution

A performance review is a great time to impress your employer. It is also a chance for you and your manager to talk candidly about your performance so that your manager can acknowledge your hard work and for you to learn what can be improved. The review should be a learning experience for both parties. It's also a great chance to talk about your goals, both in your career and in your compensation.

So how should you prepare for a performance review?

You should gather a detailed list of:

1. **Your accomplishments.** Accomplishments can include saving or making the company money, streamlining processes, or solving vexing problems. Be specific and quantify your impact with precise numbers. Quantification makes your impact more tangible.

2. **Areas of improvement.** Take initiative by listing areas of improvement. It shows your employer that you want to learn and grow. Perhaps your sales were lagging, or you didn't have the right skills or expertise for key projects. By explaining how you plan to improve, you show initiative and that you're willing to take responsibility for your progress.

3. **Ways the company can help you be more productive.** Your employer wants to help you be the best employee you can be. Identify roadblocks to your productivity or your goals. Perhaps you might want to ask for expensive statistical software package that reduces dependence on another team. Or propose hiring a new employee who can assist with repetitive tasks.

4. **Short and long-term goals.** Setting goals clarifies expectations on what will be achieved in the coming quarter or year. It's also an opportunity to check for alignment with your boss' and the company's overall objectives.

5. **Changes you want in your compensation (if any).** If you think that your compensation is inadequate for your work, ask your manager for a raise. During the performance review, you'll have put in the hard work recalling and explaining your accomplishments for the year. This is ammunition that you need to justify a salary increase.

Take a look at Resources D and E in the Appendix. Resource E gives three examples of performance review evaluation forms that your employer might use.

Resource D is a candidate side worksheet that's very similar to a performance review evaluation form, but more suited for informal scenarios to help your manager to defend a raise or promotion request.

## Sample Person-to-Person Script

JANE: I would like to start off by talking about my accomplishments this past year. I exceed my sales quota by $230,000 more in sales and generated the largest number of new leads on the team. I also pioneered the shift towards our new sales tracking system, reducing time spent on month-end sales reporting by 40 percent.

MANAGER: Great! You mentioned the biggest achievement that was on my list along with one that I wasn't aware of. Thank you for reminding me of your great work.

JANE: You're welcome.

MANAGER: Do you have any areas of improvement you would like to discuss? You can tell me what you think first and then we'll see if our lists match.

JANE: First, I think that I need to work on my communication skills with colleagues. I sometimes forget to update them on changes, and I have seen instances where I had caused trouble, notably with the Blue Granite account.

Second, I need to delegate more effectively as a manager. I often find it easier to get things done myself. I just hate wasting time explaining things to others, watch them mess up, and clean up the mess afterward. However, I do see how my behavior is alienating the team.

Third, I need to appreciate my team more. Sometimes I get so caught up with the latest deadline that I forget to acknowledge and celebrate their wins.

MANAGER: That's a good list. There's one more thing I'd like to add: setting and communicating goals. Until you mentioned it now, I had no idea that you initiated the shift to the new sales tracking system. While I appreciate your work there, we could have had the business analysts lead that work, freeing you up to acquire new customers.

JANE: Thank you for feedback. I made a mistake there. I'll work on apprising you of my objectives and status in our weekly one-on-one meetings going forward.

MANAGER: Is there anything that the company can do to make your job easier or help you be more productive?

JANE: Actually, I did think of some things while I prepared for the review. My computer inhibits my productivity. It's slow and often randomly shuts down. When I called tech support, they said that nothing was wrong with the computer. It is just too old.

MANAGER: Oh, that's interesting. I'll take ask our team admin to address this for you.

JANE: Thank you. I think it would also be helpful if we talked about short and long-term goals and try to sync up our expectations.

MANAGER: Go ahead.

JANE: My short-term goal is to generate an additional $40,000 in revenue in the next year. My long-term goals are mostly managerial related. For example, I want to clearly show my team that I value their hard work. Also, I don't want inhibit projects with my lack of communication.

MANAGER: Sounds like a good start. Let me give your goals some more thought, and I'll see if there's any others I'd like to add. Before we wrap up our meeting, is there anything else you want to talk about?

JANE: Actually, I would like to discuss compensation. I would like to request a one-time $3,000 bonus, based on my accomplishments this year.

MANAGER: You did beat your sales quota, and you've been quite the thought leader in our organization. I'll send your request to upper management. Could you send me your notes for the performance review? It'll be a helpful checklist as I recount your achievements to my boss.

JANE: Thank you very much! I'll send it right away.

## Sample Email Script

*This section has been intentionally left blank, as we do not anticipate a performance review occurring via email.*

## Case 58: What to do if I want to have a say in which projects I receive?

### Story

Jane has been overwhelmed lately with a large number of difficult projects. Because she was unable to meet all the deadlines, she became ineligible for a third of her bonus. When she asked her other coworkers, she found that they all had the same number of projects. However, her projects were more complex and difficult. Jane became frustrated because of the inequity. The projects could have been divided in a way that gave everyone equal work.

She doesn't want to be in a similar situation again next year.

What should Jane do?

### Solution

Jane should talk to her boss about this issue. If her manager cannot split the projects evenly, then Jane should be able to have a say in choosing her own projects. Also, she should not assume that her manager had maliciously chosen difficult projects for her. That attitude might lead to hostility and damage her relationship with her manager if negotiations become adversarial.

### Sample Person-to-Person Script

Jane: Hello, may I talk to you about my projects this year?

MANAGER: Of course.

JANE: As you're aware, I did not meet my project deadlines this year even though I had the same number of projects as my other colleagues. I noticed that their projects were easier than mine. Were you aware that my projects were more difficult?

MANAGER: Actually, I wasn't. I thought that the projects were quite similar in difficulty and effort required.

JANE: I would like to respectfully disagree. For example, while the estimated time for the projects seemed the same, my projects actually required more time. My projects required setup time, while my colleagues' projects did not.

MANAGER: I see.

JANE: I find it a little unfair that I had received more difficult assignments, especially my projects performance impacts my year-end bonus. Because the projects could not be completed on time, I will not receive a third of my year-end bonus.

MANAGER: I see. I will be more careful about assigning more equitable projects across the team.

JANE: I would also like to review which projects I receive.

MANAGER: It's not customary for employees to choose their own projects.

JANE: I understand that it is unusual. I re-read company policies, and it does not state that employees can't choose their own projects. I'm not asking to have the final say in which projects to work on. Instead, I would like to review the project list and request certain projects.

MANAGER: What if I extend the same privilege to your colleagues? There would create an inordinate number of steps to the current process.

JANE: In exchange for this benefit, I'd do a few things: run the weekly team meetings, send notes after the meetings, and run the quarterly budgeting process.

MANAGER: You would rather take on all these responsibilities in exchange for the privilege to choose your own projects? It seems like a lot of work.

JANE: I appreciate that you recognize that I'm taking on more work, but quite honestly, I feel the three additional responsibilities is manageable. It'll also free up your time to work on more strategic initiatives.

MANAGER: That seems fair. Hopefully this way we won't run into the same project equity problem.

JANE: Thanks for accepting my proposal.

## Sample Email Script

Dear Manager,

I would like to talk to you about my projects this year. As you're aware, I did not meet my project deadlines this year even though I had the same number of projects as my colleagues. When I looked into their projects, I noticed that they were much easier than mine. For example, while the estimated time for the projects seemed the same, my projects actually required more time. My projects required setup time, while my colleagues' projects did not.

I find it unfair that I received more difficult assignments, especially when they are tied into my bonus. Because the projects could not be completed on time, I will not receive a third of my year-end bonus.

That is why I would like to request being able to have a say in which projects are assigned to my roster. I understand that it is unusual. However, I reviewed the company policies, and it does not state that employees can't choose their own projects. I'm not asking to have the final say in which projects to work on. Instead, I would like to review the project list and request certain projects.

I do not want to run into a similar problem again next year, so I hope that this change will prevent this situation.

Thank you,

Jane

## Case 59: What should I do if my manager gives me floundering sales accounts?

### Story

Jane started working as a sales executive at a well-respected company. 70 percent of her total compensation is based on the customers in her book of business.

She enjoys working with her clients, but lately she's been receiving very difficult sales accounts. Many of the sales accounts have languished; others have been marked as recurring clients when they haven't purchased products.

Jane would like review new accounts added to her quota before accepting. However, her manager is simply assigning accounts without review. He's deflecting her review requests and putting her on the defensive, claiming that she's not capable of doing her job.

What should she do?

### Solution

Don't feel compelled to react to or reject criticism. Instead, explain why you feel the way you do. Explaining your motives fosters trust in a relationship and can be used to your advantage. Also take care to not attack the other party when negotiating.

### Sample Person-to-Person Script

JANE: For this coming fiscal year, I'd like to review the list of customers before getting them assigned to me.

MANAGER: We don't allow new sales executives to review their customer list.

JANE: My commission is based on whether or not I can meet my quota. One of the biggest drivers to performance is account quality and potential.

MANAGER: Come on, this is sales. You, better than anyone, should know that there's some risk involved.

JANE: I can accept risk, but I'm entitled to researching the accounts before I accept it. If someone asked me to jump off a cliff, it'd be reasonable for me to check if there are rocks or water down below, no?

MANAGER: You make a good point. Okay, I'll allow you to review the list before you accept them.

## Sample Email Script

Dear Manager,

I would like to talk to you about my sales accounts. For the coming fiscal year, I would like to review my customer list before accepting them.

I feel that I have received very difficult accounts. Many of the sales accounts have languished; others have been marked as recurring clients when they haven't purchased products.

My commission is based on whether or not I can meet my quota. One of the biggest drivers to performance is account quality and potential. If I do not get a chance to evaluate an account's quality and potential before accepting, I don't see how I can get a fair chance at meeting or beating quota.

Thanks for considering my request; I look forward to hearing from you soon.

Thank you,

Jane

# Case 60: What should I do if I want to work on a specific project?

## Story

Jane has been working at her current company for four years. She has developed a friendship and mentorship with one of her colleagues, Megan. Megan is four levels above Jane and a trusted advisor to Jane's manager, Elle. Jane wants to be part of a new company project that creates fitness tracking devices, but she was assigned to another team.

What should Jane do?

## Solution

An effective, but underutilized tactic, is to build alliances with others in an organization.

In this case, Jane should evaluate if Megan can influence her manager, Elle and help Jane to get onto the mobile software team.

## Sample Person-to-Person Script

JANE: Hi Megan. May I speak to you about something?

MEGAN: Of course. What's on your mind?

JANE: I'm interested in fitness tracking devices. Do you think that I could be a good fit for the team?

MEGAN: I certainly think so.

JANE: Thank you. I think that I could help more than the average programmer. Since I worked on electronics in the past, I have more hardware knowledge than the rest of the team.

MEGAN: And you think that would be valuable for the project?

JANE: Yes, I do.

MEGAN: And you're not on the team?

JANE: No, my manager, Elle, put me on the software team. I was assigned before I could give my input. That's why I wanted to talk to you. I was wondering if you could talk to Elle and ask her to consider moving me to the other team.

MEGAN: I can definitely give it a try. I'll pop into Elle's office later today and see what she says.

JANE: Thank you. I really appreciate it.

## Sample Email Script

Dear Megan,

I am very interested in the new project regarding fitness tracking devices. I think that I could help more than the average programmer. Since I worked on electronics in the past, I have more hardware knowledge than the rest of the team, and my knowledge would be valuable. Unfortunately, my manager, Elle, put me on the software team. I was assigned before I could give my input.

That's why I wanted to talk to you. I was wondering if you could talk to Elle and ask her to consider moving me to the other team. She trusts your advice and thinks highly of you, so I think you would have more influence over her decision than I would.

I really appreciate your help.

Thank you,

Jane

# Part 4 Salary Negotiation Scripts for Recruiters and Hiring Managers

# Difficult Candidates

## Case 1: What should I do if my candidate wants more money?

### Story

Your candidate, Jane, is a recent university grad. You presented her a standard offer for software engineers with no experience: $50,000. Your reservation price is $62,400.

The candidate exclaims that this is below market rate of $70,000. You silently agree that your offer of $50,000 is likely below the market rate.

You are surprised that she is complaining about the offer, especially since she doesn't have any other offers. Jane also bragged how this company was the number one choice, saying that she "loved the team and the company's products." During the interview, the candidate told the interviewer that "money isn't important" when considering offers.

During the negotiation discussions, the candidate mention that World Global Consulting, a local consulting firm pays its new graduates $68,000. Jane tells you that if you offered her $68,000, she would definitely take it.

It is odd that she mentioned World Global. You do some sleuthing on LinkedIn, and you find that her classmate, just started a new job at World Global last month.

### Solution

It's likely that your candidate is talking with her friend and comparing job offers.

Looking below the surface, it looks like it is ego driven. Our candidate doesn't want to lose face by getting paid less than her friend.

A $68,000 salary request is 36 percent above the $50,000 initial offer. However, if the recruiter can convince the hiring manager that the market rate is $70,000 and raise the reservation price to $68,000, then the recruiter will offer the $68,000 that the candidate desired, wrap up the negotiation, and mark this candidate as "closed" in his or her recruiting scorecard.

Alternatively, if the recruiter's reservation price is firm at $62,400, the recruiter still has a good chance a closing the candidate, despite her $68,000 counter, especially since the candidate doesn't have competing offers.

I'd recommend that the recruiter counter with $60,000. It'll give the recruiter an additional $2,400 to work with in case the candidate counters.

To apply pressure on the candidate to accept, the recruiter should consider an authentic and thoughtful appeal centered on the team and the project. Acknowledge that the market rate is higher. Play it cool by staying strong; that is, the candidate is welcome to decline and wait for stronger offers.

## Sample Person-to-Person Script

RECRUITER: I've discussed it with the hiring manager, and we've revised our offer.

JANE: Great, I'd like to hear more about it.

RECRUITER: We've raised your offer to $60,000 per year, from $50,000.

JANE: That's a bit different from the $68,000 I wanted.

RECRUITER: I wish we could offer you more, but this is our best offer. We're a self-funded start-up, and this is the best we can do given our limited funds.

JANE: The new offer is still shy of what World Global is offering.

RECRUITER: If money is important to you, then I would recommend waiting for one of the big guys: Microsoft, Google, and Amazon. These guys can pay the big bucks.

As for World Global, I've talked to developers at similar consulting shops. They don't seem excited about what they do. They are either given a tiny piece of the overall product, or the client has asked them to work on something mundane that they don't want to put it on their resume.

You've had a chance to talk to the hiring manager, and he wants his team to work on projects that are inspiring and have the capacity to change the world. The hiring manager likes big challenges, and he doesn't get scared when he hasn't figured out all the pieces. He sees that in you too. And that's rarer than it seems.

RECRUITER: You've got a great opportunity with our company. Our projects revolve around iOS front-end, back-end, third-party cloud APIs, natural language processing, and artificial intelligence. I can't see too many other teams who would trust a fairly new developer with such a broad swath of CS disciplines. In fact, I've talked to some developers with 20 years' experience, and they get scared by our company's broad scope. But your hiring manager is betting on you. He believes you can do it.

JANE: You and the hiring manager make a convincing argument. I'll go ahead and accept.

## Sample Email Script

Dear Candidate,

I've discussed it with the hiring manager, and we've revised our offer to $60,000 per year, from $50,000.

The hiring manager and I wish we could offer you more, but this is our best offer. We're a self-funded start-up, and this is the best we can do given our limited funds.

If money is important to you, then I would recommend waiting for one of the big guys: Microsoft, Google, and Amazon. These guys can pay the big bucks. As for World Global, I've talked to developers at similar consulting shops. They don't seem excited about what they do. They are either given a tiny piece of the overall product, or the client has asked them to work on something mundane that they don't want to put it on their resume.

You've had a chance to talk to the hiring manager, and he wants his team to work on projects that are inspiring and have the capacity to change the world. The hiring manager likes big challenges, and he doesn't get scared when he hasn't figured out all the pieces. He sees that in you too. And that's rarer than it seems.

You've got a great opportunity with our company. Our projects revolve around iOS front-end, back-end, third-party cloud APIs, natural language processing, and artificial intelligence. I can't see too many other teams who would trust a fairly new developer with such a broad swath of CS disciplines. In fact, I've talked to some developers with 20 years' experience, and they get scared by our company's broad scope. But your hiring manager is betting on you. He believes you can do it.

Let me know if you have any questions. We hope to have you on the team.

Thank you,

Recruiter

# Case 2: What if I don't hear back from a candidate?

## Story

You are wrapping up interviews with candidates, and you found a particular candidate that you think would be a good fit for the team. She's smart, creative, and seems to be excited about the role. You send her a prompt email inviting her to join the company and wait patiently for her reply.

After four days of silence, you think you have been patient long enough. You want the candidate to accept the offer, but she hasn't been communicating with you. You're starting to think she's not taking the offer seriously.

What should you do?

## Solution

First, you should give your candidate the benefit of the doubt. After a few days, follow up with your candidate, reminding her that you emailed her an offer. Perhaps the email was rerouted to her unchecked spam folder. Maybe she had an emergency and could not check email. You can't automatically assume that your candidate doesn't care about the job. After all, she put in the effort to apply and interview for the position.

After a couple of attempts, you can decide whether or not you really want this candidate. If you do, warn her that you are going to retract the offer if she doesn't accept. If you don't want the candidate anymore, send her an email and politely tell her that due to her lack of communication, you are retracting the offer.

## Sample Person-to-Person Script

RECRUITER: I'm calling to follow up with you about the offer. Did you receive the offer in your email?

JANE: Yes, I did. I apologize for not getting back to you sooner. I had a family emergency.

RECRUITER: Oh I see. I hope everything is alright.

JANE: Yes, everything is okay now. The offer just got lost in the chaos of the past few days. But I'm still very interested in the offer.

RECRUITER: That's good to hear. We were considering retracting your offer because of your lack of communication.

JANE: Again, I apologize for that. I appreciate that you called to follow up instead of just pulling the offer.

RECRUITER: Of course. I'm glad you're still interested. Could we set up a time to talk about it soon?

CANDIDATE: Sure. Let me pull up my calendar.

## Sample Email Script

Dear Candidate,

I just wanted to follow up with you about the offer we emailed you a few days ago. We aren't sure if you are still interested because you haven't communicated with us. We would still like you to join our company, so please contact us to set up a time to discuss the offer.

If we don't hear back from you by the end of the week, we will assume that you do not want it.

Thank you,

Recruiter

## Case 3: What to do if I don't think the candidate deserves more money?

### Story

After interviewing candidates for a few months, you found an excellent pharmacy candidate.

When you sit down to discuss compensation, things start to go awry. The candidate knows that as a pharmacist, her skills are in demand, so she thinks she has leverage in the negotiation. What she doesn't realize is that you've interviewed other candidates. You feel those candidates are good alternatives with more reasonable salary expectations.

She starts asking for things that you can't and frankly don't want to give her. These benefits include a signing bonus, extra vacation days, and the option to telecommute. You want to keep this candidate, but you don't like how demanding she is.

What should you do?

### Solution

In this situation, you have two options, depending on whether you want to keep the candidate. If you don't want her to join because her demand nature is not a good fit for the company, pull the offer.

If you want her to join, be firm with her. Meet her on some of her terms, but also make sure she understands that she is asking for too much. At that point, you can tell her to take or leave the offer. This plan runs the risk of losing the candidate, but if neither of you were willing to budge, the negotiations would have stalled anyway. It is better for both parties to be assertive and clear.

### Sample Person-to-Person Script

RECRUITER: I think we're going about this negotiation the wrong way. You keep asking for things, and we keep turning down your requests. We have reached a stalemate. So what we should try now is to prioritize what you want. Tell me one thing that you want to change about your compensation package. What is the most important to you?

JANE: Alright. I guess the most important thing is that my salary increases by 15 percent.

RECRUITER: We can't approve a 15 percent increase, but we can give you an eight percent increase and a signing bonus of $3,000.

JANE: That is much less than what I'm asking for, especially without the other benefits like working from home and more vacation days.

RECRUITER: This is the best compensation package I can offer. You can accept and join the company. Or you can reject the offer.

JANE: You won't discuss this anymore?

RECRUITER: No. We have to fill this position. If you're not willing to accept, then we will move onto other candidates.

JANE: Okay, I'll accept it.

## Sample Email Script

Dear Candidate,

I'm disappointed with how our negotiation has been going. I think we have reached a stalemate where we both won't budge. That is why we're going to offer you the best compensation package we are willing to give someone of your credentials. That is an eight percent increase in the base salary and a $3,000 signing bonus. We can't honor your request for extra vacation days and telecommuting options at this time. You can accept the employment contract on these terms or reject the offer.

We hope that you will accept.

Thank you,

Recruiter

## Case 4: What do I do if my candidate can't make up her mind?

### Story

Your salary negotiations with a candidate have become drawn out and excruciatingly long. This time, it's not because the candidate is too demanding. Instead, it's because she can't decide what she wants. With the signing bonus, she wants "just a little bit more," but can't say the number she really wants. With the company car, she wants "something else instead," but won't say what. Even with the base salary, she can't articulate how much more she wants.

What should you do?

### Solution

Many people don't know what they want. For the candidate, it might be because she doesn't know what she's worth. She also might be too worried that she'll leave money on the table. She could also simply be overwhelmed by all the options. Whatever the reason, the best next step is helping the candidate walk through a decision-making process.

Ask questions that will help identify her needs and wants. That way she can prioritize what is important to her. Then help her identify the pros and cons of accepting different benefits and forgoing others. Be clear about which benefits are negotiable so she can focus on the aspects of the compensation package that she can actually change.

### Sample Person-to-Person Script

RECRUITER: It seems like our negotiations have stalled. Whenever we offer you another benefit or an increase in your compensation package, you just say that you want more. However, we can't reach an agreement if you can't be specific in what you want.

JANE: I am a bit overwhelmed by the choices. It's been a bit hard to decide.

RECRUITER: How about I help walk you through a decision-making process?

JANE: Sure.

RECRUITER: First, let's figure out what's most important to you. There's base salary, signing bonus, equity, and flexible hours among other options.

JANE: Okay, I guess $4,000 more in base salary is important to me.

RECRUITER: Okay. Well the budget for this position is only $2,000 more than what we offered, so we can't give you more than a $2,000 increase in base salary for now. What can we do for you instead?

JANE: Could I get a one-time signing bonus then?

RECRUITER: Perhaps. Do you have a specific number in mind?

JANE: What about $2,000?

RECRUITER: We can do that. Thank you for being specific. Now we're getting somewhere.

JANE: About the company car, what options can you give me instead of the car?

RECRUITER: We actually can't give you anything instead of the car. You can either use it or not.

JANE: I see. I guess I'm fine with the revised package you've presented. I'll sign.

## Sample Email Script

Dear Candidate,

It seems like our negotiations have stalled. Whenever we offer you another benefit or an increase in your compensation package, you just say that you want more. However, we can't reach an agreement if you can't be specific in what you want.

That is why I would like to help you determine what you want. If you could come to the negotiation table next time with a clear list of your priorities, I'm sure we can find an agreement. I will also be prepared with what we are willing to change and what we aren't willing to change.

I hope our next discussion is more productive.

Thank you,

Recruiter

## Case 5: What to do if my candidate wants a job title she doesn't deserve?

### Story

Your salary negotiation with a job candidate is not going well. She keeps insisting that she deserves the HR Director title because she is the next person under the vice president of HR. However, you don't think that she deserves the title because the position's responsibilities are not as extensive as a typical HR director. In fact, it is more accurate to say that the VP of HR is doing the work of a VP and a director. Also, the director title is often given to people who used to be a vice president, general manager, or director at a Fortune 500 company. This candidate was only a manager.

What should you do?

### Solution

As someone who knows more about the company than the candidate, simply explain to her that someone in a director position has different responsibilities than those listed in the position the candidate was offered. The discrepancy in job descriptions should reveal to the candidate that the director title does not apply to her.

### Sample Person-to-Person Script

RECRUITER: I'm sorry, but we can't give you the director title. It does not correspond to the roles and responsibilities for the position you were offered.

JANE: But I am directly under the VP of HR. That position is usually called the director.

RECRUITER: That is correct. However in our organization, the VP of HR does the work of both VP and director. Your responsibilities are not as extensive as those of a director. Also, we have a flatter organization. Most directors in our organization were formerly vice presidents, general managers and directors in Fortune 500 companies.

CANDIDATE: Will there be opportunities for me to get promoted to director?

RECRUITER: Of course. I encourage you to work with your boss on your career development plan so that it's clear what you need to do to be considered as a director level candidate in the near future.

CANDIDATE: Okay, I understand. Thank you for explaining the difference to me.

## Sample Email Script

Dear Candidate,

I'm sorry, but we can't give you the director title. It does not correspond to the roles and responsibilities for the position you were offered. While your position is directly under the VP of HR, our organization works differently than others. In our organization, the VP of HR does the work of both a VP and a director. Your responsibilities are not as extensive as those of a director. Most directors in our organization were formerly vice presidents, general managers and directors in Fortune 500 companies. It's unlikely that someone who was formerly a HR manager would be a director in our organization.

There will be opportunities for you to be considered as our next HR director. Work with your boss on developing your career development plan. With your talent, I'm confident that it'll come sooner rather than later.

Thank you,

Recruiter

## Case 6: What should I do if my candidate might get a better job offer?

### Story

After weeks of interviewing people to fill a new position, you finally found a perfect candidate. Jane has an exceptionally rare skillset, and her former colleagues vouch for her leadership and teamwork.

You know she's a hot commodity, but you're still disappointed when Jane asks to extend the offer deadline. She says that she's waiting for another offer and would like to review both offers before deciding. You don't want to lose her because she's perfect. You also need to fill the role soon, so losing the candidate will be a big setback.

What should you do?

### Solution

Given Jane's desirability, you'll have to be more patient than your typical candidate. Give her the time she needs to make the decision. As long as your offer hasn't been rejected, your company still has a chance.

In addition, there are two more things your company should do. First, see if there's anything you can do to increase the likelihood of accepting the offer.

Second, the company should start looking for back-up options immediately. Let Jane know that as part of the deadline extension, the company will rescind the offer if they find another suitable candidate.

### Sample Person-to-Person Script

JANE: Thank you for offering me the position, but I will need some more time to consider the offer.

RECRUITER: Do you think we can get a response in a few days?

JANE: Actually, I'll need four weeks. I am waiting on an offer from another company.

RECRUITER: Four weeks is a very long time.

JANE: Yes, I understand that it is, and it likely puts your company in an awkward spot. However, I need time to weigh all of my options.

*Recruiter pauses for a second*

RECRUITER: Okay. We can give you four additional weeks. While I have you on the phone, may I ask what's stopping you from accepting our offer?

JANE: The other company has an exciting opportunity, commercializing their self-driving cars.

RECRUITER: I didn't know you were interested in that. We actually have a project with the German government where we're helping to bring self-driving technology for buses. If you'd like, I can introduce you to the VP of that division, and he can tell you more about it.

JANE: Sure, I would like that very much.

## Sample Email Script

Dear Candidate,

I understand that you need four weeks to wait on another company's offer. I'll go ahead and grant that. We understand this is a tough decision, and we want you to be comfortable with what you ultimately choose.

In the meantime, I have a question for you: What's stopping you from accepting the offer?

Thank you,

Recruiter

# What's Next
## Final Thoughts on Getting More

Whether you are negotiating over email or phone, take the sample negotiation scripts and replace the fictitious names with names and details from your own situation.

If you are not sure which one of the scripts to use, do not forget that there is the magical one-minute salary negotiation script later on in the book.

And if you are still stuck, try our salary negotiation service at http://gosalaryBOOST.com. We would be honored to have you as a Salary Boost client; our talented team of salary negotiators will create a custom script just for you.

## One More Thing

Thanks for reading *Five Minutes to a Higher Salary*. However, our journey does not end here. First and foremost, we would love to hear from you. Please send questions, comments, typos and edits to: lewis@impactinterview.com.

Second, we have a few additional resources for you:

- **Get our popular one-page salary negotiation cheat sheet**. You'll find it on lewis-lin.com, along with salary negotiation worksheets featured in this book in editable, electronic form.
- **Sign-up for Lewis' newsletter**. Lewis sends salary negotiation articles and tips that you will find helpful. Sign-up at lewis-lin.com.

Finally, **we have a favor to ask you. Please take a moment to review our book on Amazon**: http://amzn.to/1AtUnwW. Amazon reviews are the most effective way to promote our book. They play an important part in promoting our book to a larger audience, which in turn gives us an opportunity to build better salary negotiation materials for you in the future.

We hope you loved what you read. But even if you feel there is room for improvement, your candid feedback will also help us improve subsequent editions of *Five Minutes to a Higher Salary*.

Thank you for reading *Five Minutes to a Higher Salary*. There is no time to waste. Boost your salary now.

*Lewis C. Lin, with Christine Ko*

# Acknowledgments

First, I would like to thank Christine Ko, who helped research, edit, and draft key parts of this book. I am grateful to have her immerse herself into the world of salary negotiations. Christine quickly became a negotiation expert.

I would like to also thank Belinda Ban, Karl Hennig, Bowdoin Su, Timothy Tow, and Christine Ying. They reviewed early drafts and provided priceless feedback.

I would also like to thank HRNasty.com, Jim Krouskop and Marty Nemko, who provided invaluable insights during my research phase.

Lastly, my parents, Sunin and Jason Lin, along with my wife, Jamie Hui, have earned my endless thanks for being my biggest supporters and cheerleaders.

*Lewis C. Lin*

# Selected Salary Negotiation Documents

## Resource A: Negotiation Preparation Worksheet

Use this worksheet to prepare for the initial salary negotiation.

1. Market value for this position is: $_____ to $_____

2. My initial request will be: $_____

3. My minimum salary requirement is: $_____

4. Who is the decision maker?

5. Do you have any insider information/contacts in company that can help you in your negotiation?

6. What are the other party's options if you reject the offer?

7. My Best Alternative To a Negotiated Agreement (BATNA) is:

8. My justifications for a better salary are:

9. Which benefits are must-haves?

10. Which benefits are nice-to-haves?

# Resource B: Comparable Analysis Table

Use this template to compare salaries with individuals with similar work and education experience. This comparable analysis allows you to infer your market value.

Gather details about comparable candidates using a LinkedIn search. Fill in details about their estimated salary using salary databases we discussed earlier in the book.

## Example Comparable Analysis Table

| | You | Comparable Candidate 1 | Comparable Candidate 2 |
|---|---|---|---|
| Salary | $110,000 (offered) | $105,000 (estimated) | $123,000 (estimated) |
| Position | Regional Sales Manager | Regional Sales Manager | Regional Sales Manager |
| Company | Company A | Company B | Company C |
| Job Location | Austin, Texas | Miami, Florida | Los Angeles, California |
| Years of Experience | 6 | 3 | 7 |
| Years of Industry Exp. | 4 | 3 | 4 |
| Undergrad School | Cornell University | University of Pennsylvania | UCLA |
| Undergrad Degree | English | History | Business Economics |
| Grad School | Harvard MBA | Harvard MBA | Harvard MBA |
| Previous Function | Recruiter | Sales Associate | Store Manager |

# Resource C: Job Offer Comparison Table

Use this table to compare competing job offers. Assigning a point value to each item in the compensation package makes it easier to compare multiple offers. Determining the point value is not an exact science, so just choose a number your gut says is reasonable. Go to the next page for an example.

# Example Job Offer Comparison Table

| | Offer A | A: Point Value | Offer B | B: Point Value |
|---|---|---|---|---|
| Salary | $103,000 | 103,000 | $147,000 | 147,000 |
| Annual Bonus | $30,000 | 20,000 | $15,000 | 10,000 |
| Signing bonus | None | 0 | $5,000 | 3,333 |
| Stock options | Yes | 10,000 | None | 0 |
| Relocation | N/A | 0 | N/A | 0 |
| Vacation | Two weeks | 2,800 | 2.5 weeks | 5,000 |
| Tuition | Up to $30,000 | 7,500 | Up to $20,000 | 5,000 |
| Commute | 30 min | 3,000 | 2 hours | -10,000 |
| Healthcare | Yes, but better | 10,000 | Yes | 7,000 |
| Company Car | Yes, with gas allowance | 2,500 | Yes | 2,200 |
| Career Potential | Yes | 12,000 | Yes | 10,000 |
| Total | | 170,800 | | 179,533 |

# Resource D: Candidate Side Worksheet

Whether it is for a raise or a performance review, in most instances, your manager has to plead your case with his boss, peers, or the HR partner. Making it easy for your boss to plead your case is how successful employees get raises and promotions. Use this worksheet to develop talking points that your boss can use to defend your raise or promotion.

## Example Candidate Side Worksheet

| Responsibility | Key Metric | Talking Point |
|---|---|---|
| Achieve or exceed $1.3MM quota for Midwest region in FY 2014 | Attained $1.5MM in revenue, beating goal by $200K. | Beat goal by $200K. |
| Showcase thought leadership on social media best practices | Presented to 300 people. Received 8.9 out of 10 on post-event surveys. | 300 people attended, expected attendance was 200. Received 8.9/10. |

## Other Accomplishments

- Personally closed JP Morgan Chase sale and increased revenue by 40K.
- Awarded Top Regional Sales Executive.Resource E: Performance Review Sheets

Here are some sample performance review sheets: you can fill out and use as the basis for your next raise discussion.

# Example A

This example lists three columns: competencies for the role, manager's rating, and explanation. Manager's assessment is listed on a scale of 1-5, where 1= Needs Improvement and 5 = Outstanding.

| Competency | Manager's Assessment | Explanation |
| --- | --- | --- |
| **Teamwork** | 5 | Showed great teamwork in all projects. Team members loved his easy-going demeanor and diplomacy skills. |
| **Communication Skills** | 4 | Mostly clearly communicates well with managers and colleagues. Could use some work communicating progress and when steps are completed. |
| **Customer Focus** | 5 | Always puts customer first. Explained new services to a current customer, leading to an additional $3,000 in annual revenue. |
| **Initiative** | 2 | Did only what was asked. Often needed prompting |

## Example B

Building on the previous example, this performance review sheet example includes a "Your Assessment" column. Using the same 1-5 rating scale, this extra column gives the candidate an opportunity to reflect on his own performance and see how the candidate's opinion of his or herself differs from the manager's opinion.

| Competency | Your Assessment | Manager's Assessment | Explanation |
|---|---|---|---|
| Teamwork | 5 | 5 | Showed great teamwork in all projects. Team members loved his easy-going demeanor and diplomacy skills. |
| Communication Skills | 4 | 4 | Mostly clearly communicates well with managers and colleagues. Could use some work communicating progress and when steps are completed. |
| Customer Focus | 4 | 5 | Always puts customer first. Explained new services to a current customer, leading to an additional $3,000 in annual revenue. |
| Initiative | 3 | 2 | Did only what was asked. Often needed prompting |

# Example C

Compared to example A, this example includes two additional columns: actual and variance to goal. Variance to goal is defined by this equation: (actuals - goal) / goal.

| Goal | Actual | Variance to Goal | Manager's Assessment | Explanation |
|---|---|---|---|---|
| **Complete 200 outbound leads** | 159 | -20.5% | 2 | Ran out of time and could not complete a full 200. Poor weather hampered the team's travel schedule, leading to scores of cancelled client meetings. |
| **Average 50 inbound leads per week** | 54 | +8% | 5 | Asked existing clients to refer new clients. Outreach worked, especially with the free steak knife promotion. |
| **$5,000 in closed sales** | $5,500 | +10% | 4 | More aggressive in adding on more services to increase the size of each sale. |

# Resource F: Recruiting Metrics

When negotiating, comprehending the recruiter's metrics and goals can help you understand his or her behavior and motivation. Ordinarily, recruiting metrics are divided into two categories: efficiency and effectiveness.

Generally, external recruiters are more concerned about efficiency while internal recruiters are more concerned about effectiveness.

### List of Common Recruiting Metrics

| Metric | Definition |
| --- | --- |
| *Efficiency* | |
| Time to Fill | Number of days from the day a job is requisitioned to the day a candidate accepts the offer. |
| Time to Start | Number of days from the day a job is requisitioned to the day the candidate starts the job. |
| Cost per Hire | Total recruiting and training costs divided by the number of positions filled. |
| Recruiting Cost Ratio | Ratio of costs to total first-year compensation of new hires. |
| Offer Acceptance Rate | Percentage of offers accepted. |
| *Effectiveness* | |
| New Hire Performance | Average % rating of hires after 6 and 12 months, compared to the average. |
| Manager Satisfaction | % of managers who are satisfied with the hiring process and candidates. |
| New Hire Turnover | % of hires that voluntarily quit within 12 months, or average tenure compared to all employees. |
| *Campus Recruiting Specific* | |
| % to Plan | Actual number of campus hires divided by the target number. |
| Employer Brand Ranking | Company ranking on the Universum brand survey. |
| Intern Conversion Rate | Percentage of interns that convert to permanent hires. |
| Top Schools Percentage | The percentage of hires from top ranked schools. |
| *Other* | |
| Salary per Hire | Starting wage per hire within a job classification. |
| Source of Hire | Per recruitment source, the number of applicants, hires, and |

| | cost per hire. |
|---|---|
| **Number of Applicants** | Number of applications received per job. |

*Source: Clara Moon and Lingmin Li, Cornell University School of Industrial and Labor Relations, Human Resources*

## Resource G: The Magical One-Minute Salary Negotiation Script

If you are in a hurry, this magical one-minute salary negotiation script will get you a higher salary. I won't explain why it works, but if you have read the rest of the book, you will understand that this magical script builds on all the concepts, theories, and negotiation research we discussed earlier.

Just fill in the blanks, and send the email to the hiring manager or the recruiter.

Congratulations. You are just one-minute away from a higher salary.

## Magical One-Minute SALARY Negotiation Script

Dear _____,
      Hiring Manager or Recruiter[1]

Thank you for offering me the position at _____.
                      Company Name[2]

I'm passionate about the role, and I'm excited to start.

For _____, I am looking for something closer
      Compensation Item[3]

to _____.
  Desired Value of Compensation Item[4]

Here's the reason why: _____.
           Explanation[5]

Is there any wiggle room on _____?
             Compensation Item[6]

Thanks,

_____
Candidate[7]

257

# Explanation of Fields

| | Label | Description | Example |
|---|---|---|---|
| 1 | Hiring Manager or Recruiter | Insert the name of your hiring manager or recruiter | Mr. or Ms. Jones |
| 2 | Company Name | Insert the company name | Google |
| 3 | Compensation Item | Include the item you'd like to negotiate | Base salary |
| 4 | Desired Value of Compensation Item | State your desired value for that item | $200,000 |
| 5 | Explanation | Describe why you deserve your desired goal. Be as specific as possible. | Friends at similar roles and companies are making $210,000 |
| 6 | Compensation Item | Same value as field #3 | Base salary |
| 7 | Candidate | Your name | Jane Doe |

# Resource H: The Magical Two-Minute Salary Raise Script

Here is another magical script, but for salary raises not offers. It is also based on negotiation principles and research discussed earlier. It is more detailed, so it will take two minutes instead of one. This was inspired by a similar script featured on GetRaised.com.

## Magical Two-Minute RAISE Negotiation Script

Dear _____,

Boss Name[1]

I've enjoyed working on your team here at _____

Company Name[2]

for the last _____.

Years at Company[3]

I'm really grateful for the opportunities I've gleaned and the contributions I've made to our company.

Over the last _____, I've expanded my role and

Years at Company[4]

responsibilities. I'd like to request a review of my salary so that it's competitive with the market rate.

I've included my thoughts and reasoning below.

**Increased Responsibilities**

When I was hired as a _____, my primary duties

Original Job Title[5]

included _____.

List of Original Responsibilities[6]

However, since I was hired, I have taken additional responsibilities in _____. My increased responsibilities

List of New Responsibilities[7]

is part of the reason why I'm asking for a salary increase.

## Strong Performance

With these additional responsibilities, I have consistently exceeded my goals. For example, _____.

Give Examples of Excellent Performance[8]

This is the other reason why I'm asking for a salary increase.

## Market Value and Salary Increase Request

I've researched _____ companies with similar

Number of Companies[9]

titles, responsibilities, and company size based on my current responsibilities. My research indicates that the average salary is _____, which is more than my current

Average Market Salary[10]

salary of _____.

Current Salary[11]

Based on this research, I'd like to request a _____

Percent Salary Increase[12]

increase from my current salary of _____, raising my base

Current Salary[13]

salary to _____.

Desired Salary[14]

I'm blessed to work at _____. But I do want to be fairly

Company Name[15]

compensated for my work, and that's why I've made the request today. I'd be happy to answer any questions you may have.

I realize it may not be possible to grant my raise at this time. If I can't get a salary adjustment now, can we put together a plan on how I can earn the salary increase and revisit my raise request in six months?

Thanks for considering my request,

_____

Candidate[16]

# Explanation of Fields

| | Label | Description | Example |
|---|---|---|---|
| 1 | Boss Name | Insert your boss' name | Mr. or Ms. Jones |
| 2 | Company Name | Insert your company name | Coca-Cola |
| 3 | Years at Company | Your company tenure | Five years |
| 4 | Years at Company | Same as field #3 | Five years |
| 5 | Original Job Title | Insert the job title when you joined the team | Brand Manager |
| 6 | List of Original Responsibilities | List of your original responsibilities | Execute marketing plans, manage budgets, assist with ad copy |
| 7 | List of New Responsibilities | List of your new responsibilities | Develop profit forecasts, present to senior executives |
| 8 | Give Examples of Excellent Performance | Identify areas where you exceeded performance | Increase Sprite's market share by 300 basis points year-over-year |
| 9 | Number of Companies | Write the number of companies you researched | Three |
| 10 | Average Market Salary | Average value of base salaries for the comparable job positions | $175,000 |
| 11 | Current Salary | Write your current salary | $110,000 |
| 12 | Percent Salary Increase | Desired increase in salary, in percent | 50% |
| 13 | Current Salary | Same as field #11 | $110,000 |
| 14 | Desired Salary | Desired increase in salary, in dollars | $165,000 |
| 15 | Company Name | Same as field #2 | Coca-Cola |
| 16 | Candidate | Insert your name | Jane Doe |

# Appendix

## Cheat Sheet: Power Phrases and Questions

Ever notice how some people can effortlessly get what they want, whether it is more salary or a sensitive piece of information? Much of that power lies from saying the right things and asking certain questions.

It typically takes years to figure out how to do this well. But your time valuable, so we have devised a cheat sheet of power questions you can use to get what you want, in just minutes.

### Overcoming a Deadlocked Negotiation

Sometimes, a negotiation can stall. To regain momentum, try these phrases.

- "What would it have taken for us to reach an agreement?"
- "What is your first priority in the negotiation?"

### Negotiate Without Being Pushy

When someone asks for what they want, it can be perceived as confrontational. And confrontational people can be viewed as pushy and aggressive.

There is a way to ask for what you want without coming across as pushy. We interviewed recruiters and asked them which phrases they would like to hear, from candidates, during a negotiation. We've included their responses below. There is no surprise here, these phrases are polite, calm, and casual.

- "Is there wiggle room?"
- "How willing are you to…?"
- "How would you respond to someone asking for…?"

### Determine Your Leverage

How much more is a company willing to pay you? To find out, ascertain how much they need you. We call this understanding your leverage. That is, is paying you more money better than the company's alternative? Try these phrases to determine your leverage:

- "What do you need me to do in my first 30 days on the job?"
- "Tell me more about your pain points."
- "What do you plan to do if you can't find the right candidate?"
- "How does hiring for this role fit into the overall organizational plan?"

## Reveal an Underlying Issue

Many negotiators fail to get what they want because they have not discovered a hidden yet important source of conflict. Start by unearthing the underlying issue and then go on to address it.

- "What is important to you?"
- "What are you not willing to give up?"

## Understand an Underlying Issue

In the previous section, we talked about revealing underlying issues. But that is not enough. We need to deeply understand the underlying issue too. Use these phrases to uncover the other party's reasoning:

- "Why is that important to you?"
- "Why are you not willing to give up on that issue?"
- "Just to help me understand, why is this…?"
- "I'm sorry, I don't follow. Why is…?"
- "Could you please explain why…?"

## Explore Possible Resistance

You might want to ask for something, but you are not sure if they are open to it. Find out how strongly the other party will resist your request using these phrases.

- "Are you willing to…?"

- "What would be wrong with…?"
- "Why do you not want to…?"

## Demonstrating Understanding

Sometimes, you are trying to get information. Other times, you want the negotiator feel like they are being heard. You want to do both. The first clarifies points of agreement. The second builds trust and shows that you care.

Here are some phrases you can use to build understanding:

- "What I understand you are saying is… Is that right?"
- "As I understand it, the problem is… Am I hearing you correctly?
- "Is this the problem as you see it?"
- "Will you clarify what you mean by…? My understanding is… Is that right?"
- "To summarize, the main points as I heard them are… Have I understood you?"
- "What am I missing?"
- "Is there anything about how you see this that we haven't talked about yet?"

## Acknowledging Without Agreeing

There are times in every negotiation when you do not agree with something the other party says. Instead of ignoring them and coming across as rude, try acknowledging their statements without agreeing with these phrases.

- "I'm just trying to understand. I have a perspective of my own, but let's wait on that."
- "I'm not sure yet whether I agree or disagree, but for now I just want to understand how you see the situation."
- "I understand your position. Could I explain to you my perspective?"

## Diffuse the land grab for attention

- "Here's a suggestion: I would like both of us to have an opportunity to explain how we see things. I imagine we have different points of view. But I would like to understand your perspective, and I would like you to understand mine, even if we do not agree. You can go first, and I will listen. After you are satisfied that I understand your point of view, then I would like to take a few minutes to tell you about mine. How does this sound to you?"
- "I feel like we might be rushing into things too quickly. How about you tell me your perspective first and then I'll show you mine?"

## Request more time

Not everything will sync together perfectly. If you need more time to collect more offers or evaluate the one you were given, try these phrases.

- "Is this deadline firm?
- "When is the latest that you need a decision from me?"
- "Have other candidates requested more time in the past? If so, what was the process for doing so?"

## Explaining your request

Many people forget to explain their rationale for a request. Don't make that mistake. As we explained earlier, it makes a big difference!

- "I'm asking for X because..."

# Glossary

**alternatives** Possibilities that exist outside of a negotiated agreement.

**ambit claim** Making an extravagant, unreasonable initial offer, with the expectation that compromise and a counter offer will ensue.

**anchoring** Revealing a piece of information with the hope of using cognitive biases to tip the negotiation in the revealer's favor.

**appeasement** Conceding a goal, wish or desire to avoid an unfavorable outcome.

**BATNA** This acronym stands for best alternative to a negotiated agreement. Out of all the possibilities, this is the best possible option if no deal is reached. A negotiator should not accept an agreement that is worse than his BATNA.

**consistency** Refers to an individual's need to be consistent with prior behaviors and statements. Negotiators can leverage the consistency principle by having the other party write down their commitments.

**contextual rationalization** This is a tendency to explain a person's behavior as being influenced by their external environment, not one's personality.

**contingency** Automatic approval of an agreement on the fulfillment of a particular condition or conditions.

**deadlock** A negotiation where no progress can be made.

**dehumanization** In a negotiation context, this term refers to seeing the opposing negotiator as being less than moral.

**demonization** This is a tendency to view the other side as evil. This concept is often contrasted with contextual rationalization.

**distributive negotiation** Each party views negotiation as a process of distributing a fixed amount of value. This is sometimes called hard bargaining or positional negotiation. This is often contrasted with *integrative negotiation.* Distributive negotiation is also known as zero sum or fixed pie negotiation.

**employee stock purchase plan** A company-run program that allows employees to purchase company stock at discounted prices. Meant to encourage employee stock ownership, not all companies have this program. Also known by its acronym ESPP.

**fixed pie negotiation** See distributive negotiation.

**hiring manager** The person who a job candidate would report to if the candidate accepted the job.

**impasse** This refers to a complete disagreement on a single issue. As a result, each party feels that no additional progress can be made.

**integrative negotiation** Each party views negotiation as a shared problem. This is sometimes called win-win or interest-based negotiation. This is often contrasted with *distributive negotiation.*

**Level I negotiation** This phrase signifies a negotiation by two external parties, in contrast to a Level II negotiation. Also referred to as a "across the table" negotiation.

**Level II negotiation** A phrase developed by Robert Putnam to refer to a negotiation within a party's organization to get an external deal ratified. Also referred to as a "behind the table" negotiation.

**locus of control** In psychology, this term represents one's belief that he or she can control events affecting them.

**logrolling** The process of trading issues during a negotiation. If one party values an issue more than another, they should offer it in exchange for an issue that is more important to the other party.

**loss aversion** This phrase refers to an individual's preference for avoiding losses vs. acquiring gains.

**multiple equivalent simultaneous offers** This is a negotiation technique to make multiple offers that are considered equivalent from your perspective. Doing so helps the negotiator figure out the partner's interests, priorities and expectations.

**nibbling** Once major agreement has been reached, the other party is likely to concede on a minor issue, to prevent losing out on the overall deal.

**ratification** This is the process of asking another entity to formally approve a negotiated agreement.

**recruiter** This is an individual who works to fill open positions. This process could include identifying, attracting, and evaluating candidates. A recruiter is not a person's future boss. Recruiters can either be an employee of the hiring company or a third-party contracted to do work with the hiring manager.

**reservation price** For a buyer, this is the highest price he is willing to pay for a good or service. For a seller, this is the lowest price she is willing to sell a good or service. This term is used in conjunction with BATNA, which is the best alternative when no deal is reached.

**restricted stock units** A stock grant given to employees that has restrictions. Also known by its acronym RSUs.

**signing bonus** This is a lump sum payment given to a new employee as an incentive to join the company.

**split the difference** In a zero sum negotiation, this phrase refers to an offer to divide the difference evenly with the other party.

**stalemate** This is a situation where both sides are still talking, but progress seems to be impossible.

**stock grant** This gives an employee a certain number of shares, as part of one's overall compensation. Stock grants usually have conditions attached, such as a vesting schedule or individual performance requirements. Stock grants are normally contrasted with stock options.

**stock option** This is a right to purchase stock at a particular price, usually below current market value. With stock options, employers give employees a chance to own a portion of the company and get rewarded when the company increases in value. Stock options are normally contrasted with stock grants.

**tribalism** This involves invoking group identity in a negotiation. That is, a negotiator might see their own as familiar and trustworthy. On the flip side they might view others as the opposite. This term is often contrasted with universalism.

**universalism** This term assumes that people are the same. It underestimates differences in race, color, and creed.

**vesting** A schedule which determines when employees get partial or full ownership of an asset, such as stock options or grants.

**win-win negotiation** See integrative negotiation.

**zero sum negotiation** See distributed negotiation.

**zone of possible agreement (ZOPA)** This is an overlap between the buyer and seller's reservation prices (aka each parties' worst case). When a ZOPA exists, there's a stronger likelihood that an agreement will occur. ZOPA is also referred to as the "bargaining zone," "bargaining range," and "zone of agreement."

# Additional Readings

*The 48 Laws of Power*

**By Robert Greene**

*The 48 Laws of Power* is not strictly a negotiation book, but it provides inspiration on how you can increase negotiation leverage and power through the historical examples and insights that Greene showcases.

*AngelList: Startup Salary & Equity Data*

For the salary negotiator, there are relevant and not-so-relevant parts of AngelList. AngelList is a website where angel investors can meet start-ups looking to raise money. That is the not-so-relevant part for readers of this book.

The relevant part: there is a section of AngelList where it aggregates salary and equity data for early-stage start-ups. The salary data includes roles such as developer, sales, marketing, designer, product manager, and data scientist. It also includes regions such as Silicon Valley, New York, London, and Paris. This information is particularly helpful for candidates evaluating stock option packages at early-stage start-ups.

https://angel.co/salaries

*Bargaining For Advantage*

**By G. Richard Shell**

In *Bargaining for Advantage*, Professor G. Richard Shell takes his negotiation research, tested on thousands of students, and packs it into an informative, energetic book. His systematic approach makes it easy to become an effective negotiator.

*Bargaining With the Devil*

**By Robert Mnookin**

We have all faced a difficult party during negotiations. But ever feel like you faced an adversary who was actually evil? If you want to know how to deal with challenging opponents in the negotiation process, check out what this Harvard Law School professor has to say.

### Essentials of Negotiation

**By Roy Lewicki, Bruce Barry, and David Saunders**

This book covers the essentials of negotiation. Originally an academic textbook, Lewicki et al. explore the basics of negotiation. It also explores the subtle psychology behind conflict and resolution so you know why certain negotiation tactics succeed or fail.

### The Essentials of Negotiation

**By Harvard Business School Press and The Society for Human Resource Management**

Targeted to HR professionals, *The Essentials of Negotiation* includes tips and tools to help them become effective, influential negotiators. Topics covered include preparation techniques, how to reshape the negotiation process when it gets contentious and how to influence bosses and peers.

### Get More Money On Your Next Job

**By Lee Miller**

This book is targeted to readers who are expecting to receive a new job offer. It is filled with 25 detailed tips about how to effectively negotiate a better job offer. Whether you are new in the job market or a seasoned veteran looking for an executive position, you won't want to miss these techniques.

### Getting More

**By Stuart Diamond**

*Getting More* challenges the fundamentals of negotiation. He flips negotiation conventions upside down and explores alternatives to the norm. This book is praised by individuals, schools, and businesses across the world. It is meant to be a general negotiation book, so it can help you when negotiating salary with your boss or resolving arguments with your teenager.

### *Getting to Yes: Negotiating Agreement Without Giving In*

**By Roger Fisher, William L. Ury, Bruce Patton**

*Getting to Yes* is the classic negotiation book, based on the work of the Harvard Negotiation Project. The book explores all aspects of negotiation, aiming to help readers find mutual ground in negotiation conflicts. The book emphasizes win-win situations with memorable examples, especially the well-known orange peel story.

### *Hot or Cold: Is Communicating Anger or Threats More Effective in Negotiation?*
**By Marwan Sinaceur, Gerben A. Van Kleef, Margaret A. Neale, and Hajo Adam**

Displaying anger can be effective in negotiations because it implies a threat. However, a calm threat itself would be the most effective because the listener would perceive the negotiator as poised, making his threat more credible.

http://bit.ly/SinaceurPaper

### *How to Win Friends & Influence People*

**By Dale Carnegie**

This legendary bestseller has given many people the knowledge necessary to succeed in the world. Carnegie teaches you how to do exactly what the title says: win friends and influence people. By manipulating the world around you, you can win negotiations and get to where you want to go.

*Level II Negotiations: Helping the Other Side Meet Its "Behind the Table" Challenges*

**By James K. Sebenius**

Have a negotiation that is stalling? Your counterpart might have trouble getting buy-in for the agreement. This article discusses how to solve this.

http://hbs.me/1v3dlEz

*Negotiating Your Salary*

**By Jack Chapman**

*Negotiating Your Salary* is a quick read to help you negotiate a better salary or raise. Chapman offers techniques that either a beginning or an advanced negotiator can use effectively. He also explains why salary negotiation tactics work and how negotiations can impact your professional career with anecdotes and cartoons. Quick read.

*Negotiation*

**By Brian Tracy**

This is a great practical book for those who want to learn how to apply negotiation techniques. Tracy's teachings include how to use emotion as a tool, how to prepare effectively in advance, and how to know when to walk away or put your foot down.

*Negotiation Genius: How to Overcome Obstacles and Achieve Brilliant Results at the Bargaining Table and Beyond*

**By Deepak Malhotra and Max Bazerman**

Written by two negotiation leaders at the Harvard Business School, *Negotiation Genius* looks at ways that anybody, no matter their proficiency level, can become a negotiation genius. You will learn how to negotiate from a position of weakness, counter threats and ultimatums, negotiate ethically, and more.

*Salary Tutor*

## By Jim Hopkinson

Hopkinson offers ten steps to get the salary you deserve. They are somewhat unconventional and zany, but can be effective. He also utilizes stories, graphs, and anecdotes to make learning about negotiation more exciting.

*Secrets of Power Negotiating*

## By Roger Dawson

Dawson goes against the grain by saying that finding a win-win situation is rarely ideal. Instead you should negotiate to win while making the other party feel like they have won. Dawson also explores how to negotiate via different mediums such as talking on the phone or through instant messaging. He will also teach more subtle techniques such as reading between the lines and interpreting body language.

*The Secrets of Power Salary Negotiating*

## By Roger Dawson

This book takes you through the negotiation process from the first job offer to subsequent raises. Dawson will teach you how to negotiate assertively without coming off as greedy or arrogant. You will also learn how to become a more valuable employee so that you can earn bigger raises in the future.

*The Shadow Negotiation*

## By Deborah M. Kolb and Judith Williams

This negotiation book is written specifically for women in mind. Women often lose out in salary negotiations, either leaving money on the table or not receiving a perk. Usually, women do not negotiate aggressively enough or their assertion is off putting to the other party.

CPSIA information can be obtained at www.ICGtesting.com
Printed in the USA
LVOW08s0211030816
498821LV00004B/222/P

With *The Shadow Negotiation*, Kolb and Williams teach readers how negotiate despite these societal setbacks.

### *Technologies of Status Negotiation: Status Dynamics in Ema Discussion Groups*

**By David A. Owens, Margaret A. Neale, and Robert I. Sutton**

This essay explores the differences in face-to-face communication versus computer-mediated communication in negotiation processes.

http://bit.ly/OwensPaper

### *Women Don't Ask: Negotiation and the Gender Divide*

**By Linda Babcock and Sara Laschever**

This book, while written for female readers, is applicable to men as well. Studies find that women are held back by their own hesitations to ask for what they want. This could be due to fear of damaging a relationship, not knowing that change is possible, or society's negative reaction to assertive women. This book explores the complex barriers holding women back and how society's perception of women put them in a bind. Luckily, it also explores what men and women can do to fix unfair institutions and practices. The book also explains how women can negotiate effectively given these inequalities.